MW01094182

"This State of Wonders"

A Bur Oak Book

Edited by
John Kent Folmar

"This State of Wonders"

The Letters of an Iowa Frontier Family, 1858–1861

Ψ
University of Iowa Press
Iowa City

University of Iowa Press,
Iowa City 52242

Copyright © 1986 by the
University of Iowa

All rights reserved

Printed in the United States
of America

First paperback printing, 1991

Book design by
Richard Hendel

Typesetting by G & S Typesetters,
Austin, Texas

Printing and binding by
Thomson-Shore, Dexter, Michigan

*Title page (left to right): Hugh Anderson,
Bella Williams, J. H. Williams, and
Rebecca Williams, 1865*

Library of Congress Cataloging-in-
Publication Data

"This State of wonders".

  Bibliography: p.
  Includes index.
    1. Farm life—Iowa—History.
  2. Iowa—Social life and customs.
  3. Williams family.   4. Farmers—
Iowa—Correspondence.
  I. Folmar, John Kent, 1932–   .
  F621.T48   1986   977.7'02   86-7012
  ISBN 0-87745-154-0,
  ISBN 0-87745-341-1 (pbk.)

To my beautiful sons,
   Kent,
   Tram,
   Forrest, and
   Brendan

*On the 23rd we had the quietest
and heaviest fall of snow I ever
witnessed even in this State of
wonders and it continued calm
until yesterday evening when
the wind—which was coming
from the south east—rose and
the snow began to "kelter" and
has continued to do so since.*

—Bella Williams to James
Williams, December 27,
1860

Contents

Acknowledgments

I am indebted to a number of people who have helped in many ways to bring this project to fruition. At California University, the Faculty Research Committee awarded me a reduced teaching load. William L. Beck, the Director of Library Services, helped make resources and a private work area readily available to me. In Webster City, Iowa, Mrs. Hazel Mikel at the Kendall Young Library and Charlene Ferguson and Kevin Bahrenfuss in the Recorders Office at the Hamilton County Courthouse were most generous with their time. Miss Hazel Stotts in Ft. Dodge and the staff of the public library there provided assistance. Also, Jeanne Campbell, the Head of Technical Services at Urbana University in Urbana, Ohio, generously copied important data on the New Church in Ohio. The staff of the archives at the Academy of the New Church in Bryn Athyn, Pennsylvania, were also helpful. Dr. William F. Trimble, an associate professor of history at Auburn University, also read the manuscript and offered incisive commentary.

My special gratitude goes to Louise Williams Chamberlin, James Williams's granddaughter, for her many kindnesses. I discovered the letters while teaching American history at the University Military School in Mobile, Alabama. Her son, who is also named James Williams, brought them to me one day as part of a special assignment. Little did he realize how the collection would affect my life. The Williams Collection is in the possession of Mrs. Chamberlin in Mobile.

Finally, George Hite's granddaughter, Doris Williams Ekstrom, of Duncombe, Iowa (near the site of old Border Plains, which is mentioned in the letters), has been my alter ego in Iowa. Her indefatigable assistance and interest in the project have been an inspiration.

Introduction

The history of the West and of Iowa during the mid–nineteenth
century is the story of people, especially people in families.
These people were part of a continuing westward movement.
Most were aware of their relationships with others and with the
land—always the land! Success meant struggle; the people
who survived knew that. Everyone, except for the Native
American, was a newcomer from somewhere back east. Therefore, in the wide-open spaces of the prairies, on the very edge
of the frontier, social and economic adjustments were especially important. Usually there was very little time to write
even if one was literate, so most eyewitness descriptions of the
early years were written many years later. A few collections of
contemporary letters written by common folk, however, have
survived the ravages of time and are significant enough to be
worthy of publication. The letters of the John Hugh Williams
family in the present volume are in that group. Written from
late 1858 until the secession crisis of 1861, they present descriptions of the very new and different Iowa frontier life by
one close-knit family.

John Hugh Williams was a most interesting and industrious
man. Born in Wales on March 22, 1805, and orphaned, he
emigrated to Philadelphia when he was seventeen. There he
apparently received training as a watchmaker and engraver
from Hugh Anderson. In 1832 he married Anderson's daughter, Eleanor, and a few years later they followed the Andersons
west to St. Clairsville, Ohio. There, as the Williams family
grew, John became a successful businessman. Soon establish-
ing himself as a "man of learning and of marked ability as a debater," he became active in local cultural and civic activities.[1]
He also became a leader in the founding of the Church of New

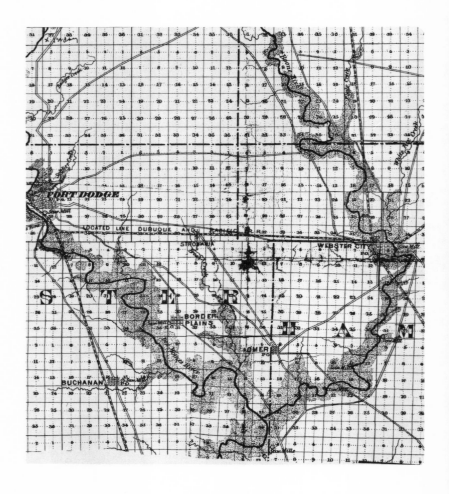

North central Iowa, 1857. Homer was located in what was then Webster County.

Jerusalem (the Swedenborgian church) in Ohio. He helped establish a New Church Society in St. Clairsville in 1847, and in 1848 he was a delegate to the New Church's western convention in Cincinnati. By 1850 he was distributing tracts in southern Ohio, debating local and regional Presbyterian ministers at the lyceum, and lecturing every other sabbath at the courthouse. When the church founded Urbana College in Urbana, Ohio, in 1851, he was named to its first board of trustees. The next year he and Eleanor were delegates to the first meeting of the Ohio Conference in Cincinnati. There he was ordained as a minister, selected to chair the missionary board and represent it on the executive board, and appointed to the publication and tract boards.[2]

In 1855, probably because of his enthusiasm for missionary work within the church, he decided to sell out and move to the frontier in Webster County in north central Iowa. In 1856 he purchased eight and two-thirds lots in the village of Homer, the first county seat, and an eighty-acre tract six miles to the north. The Williams family, which included six children, aged twenty to five, made the trek westward, and the elder Williams opened his small watchmaking shop on the corner of Third and Washington streets across from the town square. Frontier politics, however, soon drastically changed the village's prospects.[3]

Located in the center of the county, three miles equidistant from the Boone and Des Moines rivers, Homer had been attracting settlers from the East since 1853 as the leading town in the area. Rival political interests led by John F. Duncombe, however, succeeded in having the all-important government land office established in the village of Ft. Dodge, eighteen miles to the northwest, in November 1855. This faction worked with another anti-Homer element in the village of Webster City (twelve miles to the north), and after a "spirited canvass" in April 1856 they were able to have the county seat moved to Ft. Dodge. The vote was 406 to 264—three times any previous county vote! The confident Homerites had been outwitted in the art of ballot-box stuffing. These political arrangements were contingent upon the legislature agreeing to divide Webster County, which it obligingly did in January

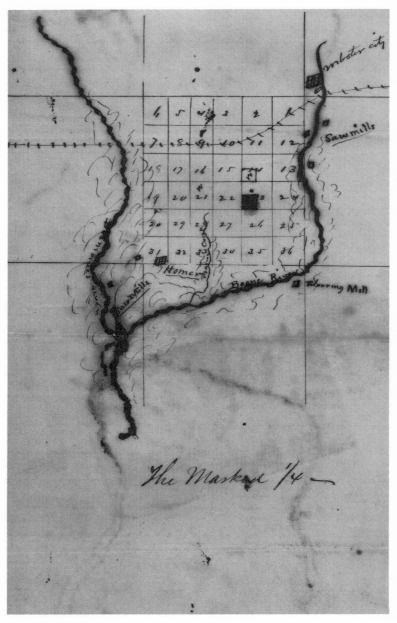

Map sent to James in 1866. "The Marked ¼" is the family farm.

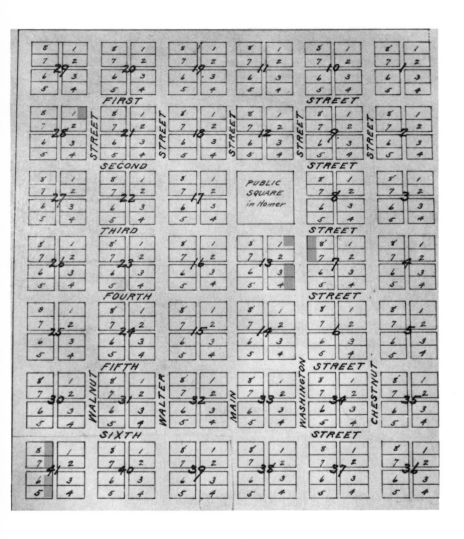

Original plat map of Homer. The Williams lots are darkened.
Source: Book 1 of Plats, p. 60, Recorders Office, Hamilton County
Courthouse, Webster City, Iowa.

1857, with the eastern half now designated as Hamilton County. Homer, suddenly located on the western boundary line of the new county, had lost the political power struggle, and the more centrally located Webster City became the new county seat.[4]

In the following year, the panic of 1857 struck with devastating effect. Immediately the debts owed to Williams at his store and his inability to complete the sale of his land in Ohio produced a tenuous financial situation for him. With money almost nonexistent, he arranged for James Madison Williams, his twenty-one-year-old son (who was also trained as a watchmaker), to help the family by moving to Augusta, Georgia, for a year to work for a friend and fellow New Churchman, Henry J. Osborne. James agreed and departed for the Deep South on July 21, 1858. With James's departure, the family began to write to him, and they continued to do so after he decided to marry and take another position in Mobile, Alabama. The letters, seventy-five in all, present a chronicle of frontier life as seen by a literate, hardworking, religious, and moral family.[5] The personal observations, impressions, reactions, and assumptions of a rather ordinary but proud family like the Williamses are not readily available elsewhere in published form. The letters also reflect a number of significant aspects of frontier life in Iowa during hard times.

Although the elder Williams often complained about the economic situation in his letters, he was essentially a small and, considering the circumstances, rather successful capitalist. Though he had purchased the lots in Homer for speculative purposes, with the economic recession he was forced to raise crops on them. He was not a merchant, but he did achieve some initial success in his small watch and jewelry shop, where he also sold trade goods—flour, coffee, sugar, and some groceries. With little or no money available, he had great difficulty in collecting debts owed to him. As the economic situation worsened in Homer, he was forced in late 1858 to move his workbench and small stock to the house.

The barter system was very important locally.[6] Williams often accepted cattle for debts due him, and he became, almost by accident, a small stockman. When he closed his shop he had fifty-seven head. It was apparent to Williams that his livestock was an important investment. His situation was, in fact, in accord with the advice of the editors of the newly established Webster City *Hamilton Freeman*, who constantly suggested that, with the availability of prairie grass and the potential for corn, stockraising should be the county's most profitable branch of agriculture.[7] In the fall of 1858, Williams and his two sons were able to cut and cure over sixty tons of hay, and the following year they cut between 125 and 130 tons, which was four times the average amount cured in the county.[8]

The season of 1860 was an arid one, however, and the prairie grass was very short. His increasing livestock herd required Williams to plant forty acres of corn and four acres of wheat and potatoes out on the farm. He had become, unexpectedly, a farmer. Unfortunately, all three crops were "light," so a portion of the herd had to be driven to market. The unexpected fluctuations in weather conditions and their impact on Williams's evolving agricultural practices and financial dealings are vividly portrayed in his letters.

When the Ohio property was sold in exchange for more land in Iowa, Williams could finally see a way out of the economic morass he had been in since 1857. In 1860 he reported to the federal population census that he held $8,000 in real property and $2,000 in personal property. This was over $4,000 more in real property than anyone else reported in Webster Township.

Another important aspect of the Williams correspondence is the picture Mrs. Eleanor Williams provides of the everyday life of women on the frontier. Eleanor Williams was the backbone of the family. Despite having a large family and being forced to spend most of her time inside the house, particularly when Mary Rebecca (nicknamed Becky) was seriously ill, she found an inner strength as farming became more a part of her family's life. Dawn to dusk work was the norm, yet in her letters she never complained about anything, except for an occasional comment about the lack of "a refined society" in Homer. Even though Mrs. Williams was ill during the spring and summer of 1859, she made no comment about it until her husband at-

James Williams, 1860.

Lizzy Rennison, 1860.

tributed it to "having too much to do to keep all in order for school."

On July 24, 1859 J. H. Williams wrote, "We are up in the morning by daylight   Ma as a general thing an hour first." And on February 19, 1860 he mentioned to James, when explaining how they got along, that "Mother is all the time (when not cooking) remodling, and repairing, 'old garments', which (aided by our wants, and astonishment) she has the tact to make as good as new." She admitted as much when she wrote on February 26 that "the children are all at school and it requires constant efort on my part to keep them in order." By then there was no longer a store in town; the closest ones were in Webster City and Boonesboro.

For her day, Eleanor Williams was well educated and literate. She read the books, newspapers, and journals that James sent to the family, and she often compared and criticized the plots of the popular novels of the day in her letters to him. More important, however, she provided a leavening contrast to the comments of her husband, who was often quite negative in his descriptions of their financial plight. In February 1860 she wrote, "Pa gave you the darkist side of the picture last week we are more confortable in some things than when you left the prospect for farming is better than it has ever been since we came to Iowa."

It is apparent that religion played a mighty roll in the everyday lives of the Williamses, even though the children seldom mentioned it. In the absence of a church, the family maintained a private altar in the house. However, Mr. Williams often spoke in the schoolhouse on the sabbath in a nonsectarian fashion as well, and his sermons attracted people from the surrounding townships. When he admonished James to put his "trust and confidence in the Lord and all will be well," he meant it. He used his church's teachings to explain human behavior and problems. In one of his long letters to James, he admonishes his son not to fall prey to "a too active '*self esteem,* and *love* of *Aprobation*'" and observes that "Our heavenly father has made us *rational* beings, and has endowed us with *Liberty*" and the ability, if we use it, to see ourselves as others see us.

A very aggressive, alert, and cogent debater of theological topics, he enjoyed any pretext to relate his religion to a topic of interest. There were few people to debate with, however, and this probably explains why he included sermonlike passages in his letters to his son, and why he often became very depressed about not having a flock of his own. Williams's background as an educated minister did give him considerable social status in the village, which in turn gave his family an entree to similar professionals and their families in Webster City.

When James was having a personal problem with his employer in March 1859, his father counselled that "To Err is 'human', to be good is angelic & to be goodness itself is Divine," because when one is born again one achieves wisdom and goodness at a higher level. Even when he was concerned about the secession crisis, John wrote that "I trust in the Divine Providence   it will pass away   the calm that will follow will be all the pleasanter, and better appreciated." The parents were, therefore, strong and moral role models for the children, who benefited immeasurably.

The lives of the children and their adjustments to the frontier are also illuminating. This is particularly important because there are few children's sources available to the historian. Despite the incredible amount of work that had to be accomplished in addition to their schooling, there was time for some leisure, both traditional and new. The family had a piano, and Isabella, nicknamed Bella, who was thirteen in 1858, was the most active musician except for James. She played the pianoforte at home and a melodeon at a neighbor's house, and in one letter she critiques a peer's performance at the piano after a visit to Webster City. She was very energetic in learning new songs from the music James sent to her, and she always shared her new endeavors with him.

Bella also collected wildflowers along Prairie Creek and planted them near the house. She even tried, without success, to grow cotton from seeds that James had sent to her. Such was the family's isolation that she did not get to visit Webster City with her father until April 1860, but what an exciting trip it was for her then. Her sister Becky, who was eleven in

1858, was ill for so long that she could not leave the house for months. She did recover, however, and in June 1860 she and Bella donned old dresses for a swim in the Boone River.

Predictably, the boys' leisure usually combined work and play. John, Jr., fifteen, and Joseph Parker Williams, ten (called Parker by the family), helped their father, especially as the farming activities increased. On Saturdays during the school term, they cut and hauled wood from along Prairie Creek. They had their own yoke of oxen, and this, of course, allowed them to drive the oxen and sledge themselves. An occasional bout with runaway oxen only made for exciting times to these youngsters. They had their pet dogs and pet calves, all with their own names. John became very adept at trapping and hunting prairie chickens with his dog Rolf, once even bringing back a crane.

The family, or most of it, would sleigh in the winters and often just walk on the prairie, particularly on the sabbath. The most important social event described in the letters was the large Fourth of July picnic in 1860 at nearby Wolsey's Grove. Bella, Becky, and George, who was then nine, attended and "they all looked very pretty," according to their mother, and "it was amuseing to see the little country children contending for their hands in the play." Where were John and Parker? They went hunting all day and returned with six prairie chickens!

As the economic situation improved in the fall of 1860, J. H. Williams's letters took on a more positive tone. The family spent Christmas day with their neighbors, the Smiths, where they enjoyed a turkey for dinner, had a taffy pull later, and played games until ten o'clock. They then, according to Bella, "waded home through the snow, to a cold house and tumbled into equaly cold beds, slept till five, and then tumbled out again to go through the daily rotine." In February 1861, Bella and Becky accompanied their father to Webster City for a dinner party at an attorney's home. Their isolation was gradually beginning to end.

Education permeated the lives of the family. J. H. Williams was the president of the local board of education and played a

George Williams (left) and John H. Williams, Jr., 1915.

major role in the rather precarious educational process within the township. James had apparently received an excellent education, and his letters to the children, particularly Bella, were often used as composition and grammar exercises. During the winter term of 1858−59, which began in November, four Williamses attended school. Becky was too ill. Bella, from the first the star pupil, wrote to James that she was "trying to learn all I can." With all of the children in school, their father had to do most of the chores. "Mother and I attend to everything," he wrote, but he added that the school had "removed the greatist source of uneasiness we had." According to Eleanor, E. H. Blair was "a most excellent teacher," and the school was the "best school they have ever attended." The spring term, which began in April, was six months long with a two-month vacation.

Teachers were very transitory on the frontier, and Blair soon moved to Webster City to teach. J. H. Williams could only lament that "we hope to have the school continued." The search began for a replacement, and he wrote to James suggesting that he consider coming home to teach. The pay was thirty-five dollars per month, with classes held six hours a day, five days a week. However, by November 1859 the board had hired J. J. Miller, an M.D. There were only thirteen scholars according to Becky. The subjects were basic: arithmetic, geography, reading, writing, and spelling. Bella also studied philosophy and grammar. John had decided to drop out for a while; he preferred to work on the farm. By April 1860, Parker had dropped out too, apparently because of poor health. After the usual summer vacation, the term continued in the fall from mid-September until mid-November. During the school term, Becky described her typical day: "George and I would get up about six oclock, eat our breakfast, then help to milk, get ready and go to school. Then about four in the evening run home, and if you were passing about that time you would see a litle boy and a girl with spy glass in hand mounting the house top and look over the prairie's to see which way the cow's, were, then booth come down and away after them and return about sundown with a drove of cattle." There was no money in the treasury for the following winter term and Dr. Miller departed. Bella soon heard a rumor that she might be chosen to teach if she would accept a delayed payment of her salary, and in her letter to James dated March 25, 1861, Becky noted that Bella was a "school marm" with twenty-five scholars.

Yet another important subject in the letters is the reaction by the local community to the discovery of gold in the Pikes Peak area of Colorado. With hard times, this seemed very attractive to many people, and the residents of Homer were no exception. In February 1859, J. H. Williams compared the likelihood of success in the gold fields by the "Fifty-Niners" with the cattle business in Iowa. He concluded that at home one would make "more gold in five years than the most successful digers will clear." A number of residents left Homer for Colorado in the spring, and some continued on to California. They were, he wrote, reckless and "if unsuccessful would [be] ready to become highwaymen."

The next month he noted that the Pikes Peak fever was widespread in Homer. Again he predicted no success by those who went, noting that one returnee said that flour was thirty dollars a sack and that he had not tasted bread for three months. In April, Williams again discussed the topic, indicating that only the shrewd would make money there. More important, he wrote, "it is entirely over looked, by the excited I might add ignorant beings that are runing a way from this state, in quest of Gold; there is more gold, in the green carpet which covers these extended plains, than can be obtained from any mine in California, or Pikes P." As an aside, he correctly predicted that "California will no doubt make a fine state not so much because there is *Gold,* there as because a large portion of it is well suited to agriculture, and manufactures may be successfully prosecuted."

By January 1860, Becky was predicting that "we will be left a lown next summer for there are so many people going to Pikes Peak." Most of the people who had gone the previous spring had returned. Two months later, Becky described how a number of local families were preparing to make the seven-hundred-mile trek. She wrote: "They get a yoke of oxen and a wagon then load the bed wih flour and provisions. then they put a nother wagon bed on top of that extending out ovr the wheels. in this way they have their bed and a little sheet iron stove to cook on with a pipe out the cover and the cover is high enough to stand up in." In November, Bella wrote that two more "Peakers" had returned "as poor as could be wished." Rumor had it that they had committed a "penitentiary offense" against a colleague, who as yet had not returned. It is apparent that, as Williams had predicted, most of those who went to Colorado were condemned to failure.

One would hardly know that the sectional controversy was occurring from the early Williams letters. Although the Webster City *Hamilton Freeman* was vehemently Republican, the Williams family was almost totally apolitical. Politics is not mentioned until late May 1860, when Mrs. Williams and the family indicated that they were amused at James's increasingly strident pro-Southern comments. Her report on the local political situation was that (1) Bella, the politician of the family, wanted a Republican president; (2) "Pa takes it very easy and there is no excitement here"; and (3) the Democrats had met in town to select a delegate to the state convention in Des Moines.

In late November, after Lincoln's election, Bella's reply to James's statement that the days of the Union were numbered was, "Granted but not '*few* and numbered,' I hope." Her father wrote a long missive in early December in which he deplored the possibility of the dissolution of the Union. A student of history, he correctly predicted that "You will not be surprised then when I say I have little faith in the political Segacity of those who look for a peaceful secesion. . . . When and where has a great nation been Sundred and such results followed? As well expect family peace and prosperity amid family broils and contentions?"

By mid-January 1861, when the Deep South had already seceded, Bella could not resist chiding James for not wanting to hear opinions contrary to his own, "for it is the *inevitable result* of slavery. to produce a domineering spirit." Later she apologized to him. In February she wrote that there was increasing interest "even by those who never manifested any interest in the afairs of the country before." On March 10 her father, not having heard what Lincoln had said in his inaugural speech six days before, wrote that secession "belongs to the past, for which he is not responsible but I fear that madness will rule the hour!"

When the Civil War erupted, the Williams family, a non-political Iowa frontier family that had been largely isolated from and immune to the developments that had led to war, was inevitably forced to make the hard choices chronicled in the letters included in an earlier volume, *From That Terrible Field*.[9] James served in the Twenty-first Alabama Regiment and John and Parker in the First Iowa Cavalry. As described in the Epilogue, the war brought changes that affected the lives of each member of the family.

Editorial Format

I have identified most of the people and locations in the letters. If not convinced that I have the correct identification, I have not attempted to provide it. I have not corrected spelling, but abbreviations, such as "no.," "qr.," "acct.," and "cr.," were spelled out in brackets. Ellipses are used where the letters are incomplete or torn.

"This State
of Wonders"

ONE

"Iowa never looked more delightful"

[Homer's] location is on a swell of land overlooking the vallies of the Boone and Des Moines Rivers and is a lovely site for a small town. It is more than one hundred feet above the bed of the former stream and four or five miles from it. It is three miles from the Des Moines and eighteen miles below Fort Dodge on the stage road from that place to the capital of the state.

—Webster City *Hamilton Freeman*, June 30, 1860

James, the eldest son, had just departed the prairies of Iowa for the Deep South. He planned to stay for a year in an attempt to help his struggling family. Predictably, the first letter written to him is by his mother, who has a little more time in the house.

From Eleanor Williams

Homer Hamilton Co Iowa
August 9, 1858

Dear James

We were so very glad to hear from you as you moved along [to Georgia]   have received three letters   after you left we felt so lonesome   we thought we could not have you so far away though our better judjment told us it was for the best it cheers us to hear from you.   you must remember we were lonesome before but are doubly so now.

I have no doubt you will succeed if you can stand the climate and the confinement   all that we hav heard in regard to the former has been favourable which makes us feel easier.

Little Rebecca keeps very feeble[1]   some days a little better and some worse   we thought she gained a little but this two days she is hardly out of bed   I think she cannot gain strength while it is so warm   we have never had such weather since we came to Iowa [in 1856]   have not had any heavy rains for one whole week   previous to that it rained almost constantly   Pa feels a little more encouraged   business has been a little better   nearly all the flour has gone out and if it continues dry we may have some grain in the country yet.   between work, sales [at the store] and flower he has taken about three hundred dollars.   He has declined trading with Day we have concluded it is better to remain for a time and perhaps there will be a better opening   if we made that trade our money obligation would be increased   we have not received any money [owed to us] from Ohio and it is very possible we will not[2]

Pa received a letter today from Mr [Henry J.] Osborne requesting you to be there on the tenth   from the spirit of his letter I think you will be pleased with the situation   I hope you will.   but my dear son we must not depend on our own strength to keep us from evil but constantly look to the Lord to bless us and keep us.

Your Mother

Rebecca says whenever she is strong enough she will write to James we are all well

I forgot to tell you Bella has played [the pianoforte] every sabbath and succeeded better much better than we expected [She] has learned five pieces well enough to play in public[3] the children send their love to you

We opened Grandpa [Anderson's] letter and inclose it in this

From Eleanor & J. H. Williams

Homer
Hamilton Co Iowa
August 19–1858

Dear James
We heard from you at Cairo and Memphis but have not
heard from you at your place of destination   we long to hear
your first impression of your new home.   it is not to be expected it will be without any alloy.   when I read your letter
from Cairo I thought among our many discomforts the one
comfort of plenty [of] pure air is ours, one that cannot be
two highly estimated.   the sun has been very hot and would
have been very oppressive had it not been for the prairie
wind.   there has been some very severe thunder storms
John Dalleys house was struck[4]   the stove pipe torn to
peices and the wall broken but none of the family were hurt
    Homer is improveing a little   Mr [William L.] Church is
building a two story house where the old log house stood[5]
Burkley is fixing up his house for a tavern and putting up
quite a large barn   Mr. [H. C.] Pemberton has the frame
of his addition up and [Hiram] Chancey his[6]   we have the
cover over the well which will add to our comfort.   the public square is fenced and looks much better   the trees are
doing well   your moss is covered with blossoms   it is beautiful.   the [sorghum] cane is ten feet high and as thick as it
can stand   it is the only thing that seems to flourish[7]
    Pa has gone out to [Benjamin] McFeeters to attend that
suit[8]   they have brought suit for the horse.   I am staying
in the store.   sometimes when everything is discourageing
here I feel glad you persevered in going, then again when I
feel more selfish and lonesome I would rather you had staid
you do not know how much we miss you   something tells
me you will be happier there, because you will have a kind of
work that suits your disposition and I trust more conjiniol society   you cannot be two careful about your companions but
the Lord alone can guide and direct you.   you must not fail
to look to him constantly

Poor Rebecca gains very slowly [and] is not yet able to walk as far as the store   the boys have hauled her to Church every sabbath but one since you left.   Mr Prescot was out to hear one of your Pa['s] sermons and in the afternoon tryed to show that there is no spiritual sense in the Word but he had the wrong side of the question and of course failed   All join in love to you

Your Mother

Dear James   tho much hurried I will take time to add to the information mother has given you, that, that suit is over, and that tho the brotherinlaw swore that I agreed to pay for the mare, that he was too willing a witness and over shot the mark.   It is a part of divine order, that evil should be blind

We are looking daily for a Letter from you after your installation and oh how anxious do we look!

Remember me to Mr Osborne and tell him I will be very glad to hear from him

Look to and put your trust and
confidence in the Lord and all
will be well
Your Affectionate father
J. H. Williams

From Columbus Pemberton

Homer Hamilton Co Iowa
Aug 25th, 1858

Friend James

Now that I suppose you have arrived in Georgia I will write you a letter   It shall not be a vehicle of idle flattery and vain protestations, but it shall be a letter full of those tender feelings that fill the heart of your unworthy but uncompromising friend.

Th'o you was never wearied with elaborate Eulogies: tho

you were never tortured with useless and vain harrangues upon your many virtues, yet your friend appreciated them all and sometimes when his soul was bowed down and full of sorrow; and the devil was raising Hell with my social relations, your presence would avenge me of Mine advasaries.

But where are you to day, and what are you doing? Ah! My boy! Transplanted from thy jenial home, seeking for safety in a strangers care is the echo that responds to my friendly call.

James, I miss thee at morning at noon and at night. I miss you at the old checker-board and in my lonely walks. I miss you and your old powder can bobbing up and down in prarie creek[9] I miss you as I pour my unering fire among the fugative [prairie] chickens that still hover around the borders of our town. I miss you more than all, because you was my friend. But to be brief, for that must be the distinguishing feature of this epistle.

. . . let that be as it may she [the weather] is a pretty fond way of giving us a few lessons in Hygene for the next 12 months to come. But what if we do fail to secure a crop chickens are plenty. like [Oliver] Cromwell I'll trust in god and keep my powder dry. Dick Fisher was down week before last and brought 1 sack of shot 2 cans of powder and caps in proportion[10] when he went home he had nary shot, part of them sown upon the prarie part of them having been dissected from the slain chickens upon our dressing table and the remainder lodged in the tough carcass of the old roosters to serve as ballast in case of high winds.

Since you left I have visited Webster City & Ft Dodge [and] seen Miss Smith and after visiting her school was ready to exclaim like Phelix to Paris "Much learning etc." I am now in the office learning the misteries of broken bones and collapsed constitutions I am now reading Surgery. Will start to College about the 25th of October the lectures will commence on the 4th of November; Mrs. [Caroline] Porterfield went to work the other morning to produce an abortion and along in the evening sometime she squeezed out a little

plug about the size of a fat oyster[11]   Instead of the wicked-
ness of the parent being visited upon the head of the child the
Lord has rested them upon her own. . . .

There is more sickness than when you left and in the absence of [a Dr.?] I have just prescribed in a case of intermit-
tent fever, Wherein old Mother Bromiley appeared for the
plaintiff and a good constitution with an argument of 200 lbs
of pure ile for the defendents.   Tis very cold for Aug.   had
to get up in the night and spread on more cover.   feel very
comfortable this morning with my winter clothing on.   have
a fire burning in the office which is just beginning to attract
the flies from the ceiling.   Reolf has just been round to see
me this morning in company with that hopeful Son of his
now they start off.   have stopped to form the acquaintance
of another dog.—   All 3 have started off to perambulate the
public square together.   The Democratic and Republican
nominees for Congress addressed the Citizens here on the
evening of the 18th.[12]

Our town in proportion to the number of inhabitants is improving more than any other town in the State. Church has
erected a fine 2 story building 18 × 30   the first dwelling
of the kind in Homer. Chancy is putting up a fine house
[James] Hartman is building a splendid house[13]   your Pa
has erected a building over the well. And our folks are building a 24 ft addition by way of the well. The public square is
fenced and by next summer I think we will be able to complete the town and then I move that it be took in to preserve
it from the ravages of time

Those Men who hauled your fathers goods sued him for
the loss of the hoss they killed on the road but failed to make
out their case.   Wesseroy was Att[orney] for plaintiff
[William R.] Daniels for def[endant.][14]

Last evening I took Snyder & Dr[ove] buggy and in company with Miss Delia Moring had quite a ride round town
Delia is pretty and knows one or 2 things but among the
girls I love Miss [Drisilla] Swanger has a place   I do think
she is one of the finest girls in the place[15]

Mary Hartman is in town, says since you left she can't bare

6

to live in the country and that your absence makes town look very uninteresting   She is I believe over to your house all her time so great is her regard for your family   But of all the girls Serepte [Tucker] is the one[16]   As my profession will require some traveling I believe I shall Marry her   as they say the d——d animal rides first rate   Ybr'gh and Serepte have been gone to Chicago 2 weeks.   will be gone Hannah says 3 weeks longer.

M[?] is gone to Webster City to stay a few days with Mrs Berkely   Miss Smiths school was out 2 weeks ago but they employed her for another term   Bella plays upon the Mellodeon   will make a good performer when she gets older.[17]

Old Man Wells pitched into your father the other Sunday and gave his doctrines hark from the tombs.   but now I will bring my letter to a close and submit it to you my friend.

J. C[olumbus] Pemberton[18]

From Bella & J. H. Williams

Homer Hamilton Co Iowa
Sep 13 1858

Dear James

Rebecca received your letter day befor yesterday but was to sick and week to answer it   indeed she has not been able to sit up for a fort night untill yesterday she sat propped up in a chair   We think her [to be] improving very fast.   we have felt affraid you would be sick but now it is getting cooler I suppose the danger is less

We have had some frost and the prairie has exchanged its covering of shineing green for the more sombre hues. The wind has been higher this few weeks past than it has been for a long time.   more like the first fall we were in Iowa.

The wild fruits have all failed but there is plenty of nuts. the boys went with the wagon a few days ago and gathered a great many

Several families have moved in this fall.   a family by the

name of Clark stoped in the little house by the barn untill they mooved a log house from town.

you remember the house used for a shop on Churches lot. to there land on the other side of that big slough which we cross in going to our farm[19]

The public square is fenced and the cotton woods you planted at our corner look quite like trees   it seemed as if we could see them grow.

There are several buildings going up in town   Mr Chaney is building on his lot   Mr James Hartman opposite us and Mr Church is building a two storey ad[di]tion to the tavern.   they had a house warming fryday befor last and the young folks are unbounded in ther praise of Mrs Church and sister   even Mrs [Electa] Smith joins them[20]

We send our love one and all to you   mine in particular

Bella

PS   Ma says for you to take care of your self when the weather changes and she thought it would be well for you to put on your overcoat when the rest do   Miss Hartman has been helping us while Rebecca is sick and she wishes to be remembered to you

There is nothing killed yet with frost   An abcess formed in Rebeccas abdomen & broke at the navel & strange as it may appear she bids fare to get well notwithstanding the contents of the bowels   we discharged it for a week. The natural course is now restored and we hope the best—tho she is a perfect skeleton. She looks bright [and] better than for weeks & her voice [is strong?] . . .

[J. H. Williams]

From J. H. Williams

Homer Oct 3 1858
Sabbath ½ 2 P.M

Dear James,

I have not spoken today [in church] and am not tired from that cause, but very much so from working at, and attention to the haying. The fall is fine, and two weeks have been very buisily spent in preparations and in geting up hay. And the comeing one if dry as it promises to be will be spent in the same way. In that case will have 100 tons   about 60 now, About 15 tons in the Barn   one Rick 120 feet and two others 45 & 60 feet   all fixed as racks so that sheep or cattle feed themselves and are safe from storm and cold at the same time. I wish this idea had occurd before the barn was built. The cost is comparatively small, & the trouble of attention to stock all most nothing. They can be turned in and left to take care of them selves   we cut the grass so close this year that 4 & 5 loads a day are brought in by the same team. It will cost me 1.25 to 1.50 a ton   last year 3 to 4.$

I know no more of the payment from Long [in Ohio] than when I first named it to you, but hope to know more soon. Should no money come from that quarter, our hard work & expenditure in getting hay will, or may be a loss. I thot it best to venture as it would be too late to get the hay after settling that question. And I must do something if we stay, and the stock buisiness is the only way I see to do it

Rebecca continues hopefully better tho improvement is very slow. The abdominal abcess still discharges, and may be the outlet to disease that has laid such strong hold upon her constitution   She eats well gains flesh, has not looked so well since my return from Ohio—[21]   begins to recover the use of her limbs, and to walk a little; but is much bent, so much so, that we sometimes fear that it is assuming a chronic form; and that if she does [get] over it, that she will always be a cripple. But she is young and we hope the best—   she may out grow it

Your letter to ma of the 19 ult is recd, also "lots" of

[news]papers to that date. They are useful to us all, particularly to the children, but I fear it is costing you too much

I dislike that idea of working at the south light very much. It was that, which nearly put me blind. I worked closely in that light, from [18]29 to late in the year [18]33. I am not yet over it, but till 1840 it was at times doubtful whether, I would loose my sight or not. That fact, lends weight to the reason, that you should not expose yourself in the same way. As all violations of order, entails weakness and tendency to disease from similar causes. But I am satisfied from experience, that watchwork should not be done at a Southern light,   were there no such heriditary tendency or weakness of eye I thot nothing could hurt my sight. I worked and read 16 & sometimes 18 hours out of the 24   15 to 16 was common. If you cannot get a northern light, or an eastern, I would for that, if no other reason prepare to change my position, as soon as, I could do it honourably, and to advantage

Should I succeed in geting my money I will have enough, with care, to start us all, so that there will not only be employment; but with proper care, and attention, a reasonable prospect of profit. And I never was any place so far as *the country*, and *opportunity* for *improvement* and advance is concerned that I liked so well. If I had but the means to give the children the advantages they ought to have while growing up. The way schools are I ought to be able to bring a Teacher here, then if we were driveing mercantile and stock buisiness, They ought to travel with us in our *"outs"*, no matter about the cost, only that it must be wisely looked to, that we entered upon and prosecuted a business, that would justify it.– [22]   The *Land*, and *Town property here*, would with the *money coming, prudently managed*, lay a foundation for all this. It has been too, the fond anticipation of my mind in a settlement here, to effect something of the kind–   That if some privations were–   suffered at first, they would in a short time give way to comfort, and plenty,   indeed that is so now, if the present debt was settled and I had a little clear capital to work on which I hope to have soon. But you are doing well, and I do not wish to divert your mind from what you are at; but if you saw it, and, the same attention was given to the matter, that must be given to succeed in the position you are in, I believe that not only more can be made but that it can be done with more manly freedom, and health-ful exercise

The cane looks well, seems nearly ripe   have done nothing with it yet, But will try to—

I do not know what Columbus [Pemberton] meant by writing about Mary Hartman   Ma had to have her a week Rebecca made so much washing [necessary] for a while, with all that could be done for near two weeks it was hard to stay in the house. There was so little of her, so wasted was she, that it was a marvel to us, how so much stench could be pro-duced. During the time, Mary was helping Ma, there was a Phrenological lecturer here,   as he did very well, and we have so little to excite I took Bella every night, but one or two;[23]   Mary went of course— she did not lodge at our house even for that week   None of us, admire her, and I particularly do not want such "affected gab-hawing fools", among the children to imitate, when it can be avoided

Now in what I have said in this letter as in some hints in a former one, I do not want to unhinge your mind, as you are doing well,   it is best to consider well, "and let *well enough alone*". But with you away, and the others likely to leave as they come up. All that is left me is to educate and prepare them for the "world and its Strifes". I must do that here, at a disadvantage   I find myself in the wrong place,   But could all act in proper concert, the advantages with the little means I hope now soon to have, would be great and the disadvan-tage of schools could readily be over-come and our small means be turned not only into competence, but in a little time into independent fortunes. But this is not the only, or indeed, the true aspect in which to view the subject. The question is, can children and parents get along together com-fortably after the majority of the former, and the *spiritual*, *which* is the true interest of both be promoted   The Spiritual interest is principal, and temporal is the instrumental. In some cases the answer to this question should be in the nega-

tive. The hereditary evils of father & son, are often so much
alike, that they excite & cause unhappiness. In other cases,
where there is due consideration, and affection, notwithstanding this likeness the answer may be affirmative

your affectionate father

J. H. Williams

Monday Morning [Oct.] 4th   Rebecca continues better,
The hay work is resumed for the week. If I get my money
and you think it will suit you, we will all be glad to see you
settled here. Stock and Merchandising in connection with
our little watch work, without being very confineing with
care and attention must succeed   I feel disturbed by the information that you work in a southern light. If you cannot
help it, put a thin green Curtain in the window. I did that to
great advantage. The last year I worked in that light of which
I speak   We have got the pumphouse up & John has at last
got through ceiling the kitchen,[24]   These little improvements add greatly to the comforts of our little house. I want
to plaster the Store, and house but fear to do any thing which
can be avoided till I know what Long will do, and I fear it
will be too late before I get to know this
   Save your means and fix yourself comfortably whether you
think of returning or not. If I do not get my money I will be
glad of all you can spare for a year, after takeing what is unavoidable for comfort

[J. H. W.]

From Bella Williams

Homer Hamilton Co Iowa

No[v.] 7 1858

Dear James
   I received your letter some time since but we were so busy
that I had not time to answer it   Mr James Hartman made a
mill and we pressed about half our cane but it had soured so

that Pa thought it was not worth while to press the rest   we made about five gallons of very clear molasses but it has a bitter taste that we thought was caused by the sourness of the cane and the lime put in to correct it

Rebecca can walk around better than ever since she was hurt and talks of going to school this winter

We have been going to school a week.   the teacher is a Mr. [E. H.] Blair from webster City. We all like him very well.[25] I am trying to learn all I can

I studied your letter well with the aid of a dictionary but if there was any mistakes I did not detect them

We have got our kitchen and pump house finished at last but Mr Hartman kept us climbing over his benches for more than a month

Mr Butterworth and Miss Serepty Tucker were married about six weeks ago at Mr Churches. Mr Butterworth surprised all by inviting them to his wedding supper at nine O clock.   but they were to be married at six at Squire Thistles in the country but when they got there they had no license they then sent to webster city for one   when they came back every one thought they were married until two A.M. when Mr Taylor returned with the license.   and then they had another trouble for Squire Thistle could not marrie them out of his county and they had to send after Mr [Mc]Feeters

I received the second cotton you sent me   it looks very different from what I thought it would in the pod

Bella

P S   Ma and I went to Mr Butterworths wedding but returned about ten o clock

From Rebecca Williams

Homer Hamilton Co Iowa
Nov 10– 1858

Dear Brother

I often think of you and would not know what to say first if you were to come home   I would not know what to do

All the children go to school but me and I am trying to learn at home

George is learning very fast   I expect he will soon be able to write to you

John sold Peette to Mr Alexander and got five dollars for him

Pa brought the store down to the house   he said he could not do the littel chorse that had to be attended to and have to run there

You said you would have liked to have had me along with you in the woods but if I had been with you and seen such a funny tree as that I expect I would have bothered you so that you would haved wished I was in homer

I would hardly beleave that it was an oak if I did see the acorns on it   it had such funny leaves   I would keep chattering all the time   I would like to see those pretty boys you talk about but I would rather see you with your new suit on I think if a stoave pipe [hat] becomes any body I think that it will become you

Little Janny says she wont like you if you dont come home
Rebecca

From J. H. Williams

Homer Hamilton Co Iowa
Dec 12 1858

Dear James

Your Letter of the 21 ult is recd   It gave us great pleasure and releif. We had recd nothing later than the 13th & were fearful that there was something the Matter.

I think all my letters to you are not recd as you do not notice one containing a 1.00 bill on *Southern Bank* of *Ga.*– worthless here

We are very sorry to hear of your having a cold. If you find any trouble in that way, or if you apprehend it, come home at once   do not risk any thing on that point. You are at the very age at which it should not be done. What signifies makeing a few hundred dollars! If I get my money which I hope will be soon, we will have all the property clear, and one Thousand Dollars to act on. Now with our Trade, the property and Stock all clear,   We can do well without a dollar, if we give the same attention, with less than ½ the confinement You now give and submit to. Indeed as the children are going to school, and must continue to do so. I am looseing all the time by the manner I am driven from point to point quite as much as you can possibly clear with all the care you can exercise. This loss will be greater when I get my money and increase the goods. If I go to collect, or to see Stock, I ought to trade for, or to the farm– or to lay in goods, All is shut up and neglected   But I will get along with this as best I can. I do not wish these things to controle you. I can change my position and business so as not to require the presence and care of so many. Nor will it do, to leave Matters in the care of the children however well they intend,   they are but "boys", and business but temporarily left in such hands must soon go into confusion for want of experience, and judgement, and inteligent care

I do think from what you say, and what I fear, that you will not be so clear of colds as here,   If so you ought to think of staying two or three years   The question is should yu stay . . . or if you are continuing to make as much as you have been doing, and your compensation is not correspondingly increased. Nor would I do it if you cannot make yourself comfortable and feel at home in Mr. O[sborne']s house in which from what you said in a former letter you will probaly board soon. However as to this last point I *rather feel than see*, that you may be over sensative,   But you can examine this Matter, and if so, put it away as an enemy to *true man-*

hood, *dignity* of *Character*, and *peace* of *mind*. The reason
we can examine ourselves, as well as others can, *is this*. Our
heavenly father has made us *rational* beings, and has endowed us with *Liberty*. In the exercise of these *gifts*, or *powers*. If we let in but a small degree of light from heaven, we
can seperate ourselves from ourselves, and thus view ourselves as distant objects— "see ourselves as others see us," as
an impartial eye would see us, or even as enemies see us,   In
the due exercise of this power we will find much of our unhappiness to be the offspring of suspicisions, engendered by a
too active "*self esteem*, and *love* of *Aprobation*". When human
conduct is analised how often will we find, where we think
we have been treated with neglect, and hauteur, that the per-
son has not so much as thot of us, but has been wholy absorbed in the little world within and arround them. This
power of viewing ourselves in the light of truth is confered,
that we may by the exercise of it be rendered happy here, and
be regenerated and be thereby prepared for Heaven, and happiness hereafter   Those who will not thus abstract themselves
from themselves— cannot possibly acknowledge in themselves
any evil, neither can they detect it—   They cannot be regenerated. They remain Natural, and by wicked lives make
themselves more and more *sensual*, *blind* and *Infernal*. Just
the reverse of the ascending scale opened in the man who acknowledge and Obeys the *Lord*.

. . . There are many little things I want to tell you. I have
got no money yet, and tho the number who can dunn me
are reduced still I am harrassed, and fear that every one that
comes in is after money. I have taken Long at his offer of
2100$ he paying [George] Brown but have heard no more
from him tho there is time[26]

I have made little headway in getting stock,   we have but
28 head of Cattle, 9 of them Calves, 6 Cows, 7 of the old
Oxen, 6 that will be 2 years old in the spring. I know of some
that I would go out and buy, but fear to do more till sure of
money

Money is scarce beyond any thing you can immagine   that

would be in my favor however, if I had my money   prices are becoming more and more reasonable, tho some are still too high   Bread stuffs are very scarce,   Flour 4.$ Corn 40 to 50 cts which with the scarcity of money is very high.

The Children are all very ardent in their Studies and as they have a very good and orderly school are doing well. But they should continue at least 2 years and I feel doubtful that the present teacher can be retained. Will do what I can towards it

We have had [a] close winter since the 9th of Nov   sleighing good now, and most of the time. Thermometer has been as low as 28 to 30, but not unpleasant as there has been no drifting   We have had no colds, nor do we hear any one cough. To day there is a change on hand, temperature above the freezeing point at 2½ P.M. It may result in rain and a general thaw, but by 4 or 5 P.M. it is most likely to be colder and snow,   that is the tendency of changes at this season in this Lat[itude]. We have had more winter than you will see to first of April in Ga. Still Stock & every thing does well when properly cared for.

Rebecca's abcess occasionaly runs a little . . . but that does not allarm us, as she is gaining strenght and flesh, and is straighening up. She is studying some and could go to school, but we think it best not to send her yet

We were a little surprised to hear that you are going to be a farmer yet. Nor are we quite sure that you have weighed that point well enough. Indeed to farm alone productive as the land here is, will not do. But for us to act in union, and concert, carrying on Merchandising[,] agriculture, and the stock business in two or 3 of its branches, (Cattle, Sheep, and Horses) united, would with due and inteligent care be a *tryumipant Success. Nor* need it allarm you, the amount of Capital required   When the mind enters the subject, so that the proper econemy and care is always observed, and given, Much Capital is not required. The amount at command only varies the mode of operating at first, till Capital is accumulated by industry and care. But every one who is inteligent, sees that success in buisiness, requires the cooperation, of skillful, industrious, and enterpriseing, and energetic parteners. The power to produce wealth by associated numbers which is incalculable is what is sought by the partnerships which every where prevail in buisiness. It is true they are often failures, but this occurs through defect of the proper qualities in the parties to them. The father of the Roschilds, was honest industrious and energetic. He saw the power of associative industry in action. when confidence was well placed and recomended it to his sons,   sufice it to say they followed his advice. And tho they fortune on which he started them was but moderate, they soon became the Bankers of Europe, and now are at the head of the monetory affairs of the Civilized World. Let these conditions exist—*Industry, Honesty, Cooperation, Intelligence*, and *Confidence*. . . .

[J. H. Williams]

From Rebecca Williams

Homer Hamilton Conty Iowa
Jan 6 1859

Dear Brother

For a few days I have not bean so well but I am geting beter now and can sit up and I intend to talk to you a little while on this peice of paper

Christmas has past the same as any other days, only we miss you more   it seemed as if you ought to have been here on that day

They had a party at Mr Harris's on Chrismas eve and on New Years eve at Webster City

All the snow has gone off and it was quit mudy for a few days but it has all frozen up again

Mr Dally is going away and maby Mr Walker will go in the spring but he dont know Where   Mr [George] Gregory and Mr [A.] Mesmore has taken the big store a way to Fort Doge[27]

Mr Tucker says that Mr Butterworth will build out on Bruchy [Creek] next spring and go to farming and raising stock[28]

I wish you were a little shorter or a little taller so that your pockets would miss the door nobs   how do you get along now when you have no one to mend for you

We all send our love to you

Rebecca

From J. H. Williams

Homer Hamilton Co Iowa
Jan 25 1859

Dear James,

Your letters up to the 9th inst to Rebecca is received. The draft answered very well and with what I have been able to raise enabled me to close three small claims

I will embrace the first opportunity to get the pictures you desire.   It is the cheapest external visit we can make you. In the meantime I will write as often as I can; and when the children get through with their school you may look for such "lots", of letters that you will not "think long about home", . . . tho it requires absence interferes very little with home intercourse and association.

It makes us all very happy to know that you are discharging your duty. Mr. O[sborne]'s beautiful compliment is stronger than words in your *favor*. I have no doubt but you deserve his confidence and esteem. Continue to discharge your duties and you will maintain it, and be happy. But bear in mind a man may do his duty from two sources. He may do it from the Lord, or from himself. In the external form the actions may be a like, but internally, they are as different as sound and rotten fruit, as light and darkness, as summer when all is life, and winter when all is drear and desolate, as different as the *carnal* and *Spiritual mind*. As different in a word, as Heaven and Hell. For we do not act from ourselves tho it so appears. This we may see when we reflect, but not while we act. Wisdom consists in reflecting on the motives of our actions puting away, or rejecting what is evil in them back to Hell from whence it came, and appropriating those things which we perceive to be from the Lord

I have just received a Letter from *Grand Pa*. He will be greatly pleased I know with Mr O[sborne']s and your likeness

He writes that Long has done nothing in compliance with his offer yet. I begin to fear what he Grand Pa does not think of, that he wishes to keep me in expectation till he thinks it will be too late for me to help myself   And then he will let Brown sell it on the notes I sold him;   When his friends can step in and buy it for him. If he takes this Course, It will double my liability, as I have had no thot of lifting those notes, but intended that he, or what is the same, the Land should do it. Grand Pa thinks Brown will demand his money first of April. If He does and Long takes the course I apprehend I must meet the matter some way   the sacrifice would be too great. I will know next month   his last promise is made for that time. If he fails I must appeal to you and Mr Osborne to help me out of the difficulty

No snow now for over 6 weeks   weather fine and dry,   we may say there has been no rain this winter. With the exception of two days the tempreture has not been so as in nov[ember] and the early part of Dec. We have had however about 4 days in all   one of them in this month that made me wish I was in *Ga.*. Tho if our winters were like the greatest part of this month I think I would prefer the climate to that of Augusta. *No colds here*   [Prairie] Fires all around. There is a Brillant One East now

Have increased the stock to 43– 10 since last report   All do well. We have no feeding to do but have to water. Write often no matter how short

Your affectionate father
J. H. Williams

From J. H. & George Williams

Feb 22 1859

Dear James,

I owe an appology for not writing to you sooner. I recollect promising to write often— circumstances led me to let the time pass till the reception of your letter referring to Mr O[sborne]'s letter then I put it off from day to day till it should be received. I am very buisy too. You can see I must be. I do all the chores and some watch work. So that you see I have plenty of what you would like to take a part in, of "roughing it". Indeed a little too much.

I have given a full explanation of the matters you will feel the most interest in to Mr O[sborne] who will inform you in regard to them

Georgie has written you "lots", if you can make it out. He crossed out a word which put him in great trouble. I told him to send it, he said he would, that you had crossed one in your letter to him so you were eaqueal

Emma Pemberton has presented a Grandson to her father and Mother.[29] It was not suspected till within a little time of its makeing a noise in the world. Dr. Selby has the honor. He of course some months before it was known took "*french leave.*"[30] You doubtless remember how indignant it always made me when flattering attentions to any member of the family came from that quarter. You know too how much I[t] had to vex me in that way, now you see the reason of it, True I did not just see what has happened. But experience had taught me to shun persons of such habits as I would a serpent I refer to it, because I have myself felt, that I might apper as unreasonable if not uncharitable in the eyes of the Children. As they are as worthy in most respects of any family here. Truly the state of the world is infernal as Mr O[sborne] observes

Write short and as often as convenient and some of us will try to return the favor. We often miss you, particularly on Sabbath mornings when we surround the family alter, Still we are not in consequence unhappy   We know that if you look to the Lord you are laying the foundation for a useful life. Acknowledge him in all your ways and he will direct your paths

Your affectionate father

J. H. Williams

Dear James

I would like to see you very much   we have saw three hundred soldiers go through town last fall   best of all they was all drssed a like and they had five cannons and three hundred horses and mules   [We] have 46 head of cattle and one of the cows has alittle calf   it is Reac's calf   we have ten cows   I have a yoke   John has one that he calls him Jake they all haft to write compo[si]tions but me and Rebeca but we speak   I have got [a]head 144 times this term and one of my class has nine times and the other ten times   Who gets the most   Jakne Pemberton is going to get the ticket[31] [Our dog] Rolf has his leg hort some way   I do not no how he got it hort   I ges he get it hort fiteing and he hort it Jakie has two dogs got some poison and well when we was hauling hay Pa and me went to get a load of hay   We had dick and boley and Pa would not drive them   they ran away on the wagon   ran about a quarter of a mile   John and Parker was with the other wagon   Osker Danils ran as fast as he could and caugh them   he said I looked as white as a sheet[32]   it is snowing today very hard and the gess are in the ponds and rivers.   we have tried to trap praieries chickens we have caught ten or leven   [?] . . . goes to them and takes out of the traps and leaves us some and takes the others home for his self and leaves us one or two chickens

George Hite Williams

From J. H. Williams

Dear James;

Since the knowledge of the mishap in Pemberton's Family
I have dropt my appointment.   there are but few others,
of our daily lessening population reading. We have retired
within ourselves more and more, and when tired reading, it
seems the most profitable thing I can do to hold a little conversation in a free way with you.—   Our stock continues to
do well,   we have 47 head,   will havve 6 fresh cows in a
short time   have 3 now, And will have ten when all come in.
I may get a few more on debts but do not much expect it, as
I find for the most part those who got in my debt do not intend to pay

I had another Letter from Grand Pa dated 4th inst. He
thinks Long has been only trifling in his offers   I think he
has been doing worse! He is *ignorant*, and *Cunning with
all.*   He thinks to get me in a difficulty from which I can
make no escape when his friends will buy the Land. I am
writing to [D. D. T.] Cowen to call on him, Who will bring
him to an issue.[33]   Make him give up poss[ess]ion, buy it in
earnest, or bring suit on the 4 notes due, and fore close the
mortgage. If he gives it up I will have Cowen to Advertise it
and sell it as soon as possible, but it cannot be done before
August, perhaps not so soon

Till I pay the debt off I can do nothing   it is very hard for
me to determine what to do. I have not communicated any
idea of moveing from here to Grand Pa much less that
Georgia was thot of. I know he would go in for it, but I see
that it is a matter that must be decided rationally. To be actu-
ated by an impulse will not answer. The loss that must be
submited to here, the expense of moveing, and the advantages too of this location in health, as well as for the bettering
of our condition when a little money is obtained to act on
all these things must be carefully weighed, Another matter
too is to be considered,   none of us seem to like close con-

finement, nor are we suited by physical force to the drudgery of mere farmers, but with proper attention we may succeed as stock growers The boys seem to like it, It requirs care, and inteligent attention, but not hard labor if there is a little money to start on. Young stock will double every year for 4 years, And when the increase of the young is added which begins the 2nd year, the increased value is much greater, with sheep it is much greater than with cattle and profits commence at once. In cattle it stands thus, first fall 3$ 2nd $6, 3rd $12, 4th 24.$ which is a very safe estimate as you may see, a pair of steers at 4 well managed will if made fat at that age net after paying all expenses 3 times that that is 3 times 48$ in New York. But to manage such a buisiness the united activity of several is required; The affairs at home must get the right kind of care and the affairs abroad must be managed by with vigor, Intelligence, and business tact. In every part of the operation there would be enough of the open air and of *"roughing it"*, without Slavish drudgery, or desolation of health and morrals. A buisiness like this conducted on a moderate capital will make more gold in five years than the most successful digers will clear. Indeed those who are successful will but perform the part of *"asses"*, to carry the Gold to those who vigorously prosecute profitable and useful enterprises.[34]

A number will leave here in the spring for Pikes Peak if they can raise the means. The persons that are going, will make nothing even if there is gold there in abundance. It is not got without hard Labor and exposure working in rain, cold, mud, and watter, and while in this condition uncomfortably fed and Lodged, There is a man here who was two years in California. He is a stout able bodied man He was able to work but 9 months of that time I enquired the reason, part of the time was too wet or too cold, the bal. he was sick from the exposure He washed about 1500$ and was able to leave with 700$. part of that was spent in geting here He has not a dollar now but hard as he is . . . he will let the "unfledged", go to "Pikes Peake", There are a number here who have seen the "Elephant" that too the real

"Elephant".[35] They were where there realy was gold but not one wants to go again, or make Money. If John Dally be excepted. He brought home some but the history of his case is coming to light now and is disgraceful. He married it seems and kept a Gambling House. Gathered up all he could including his wifes watch and Jewels and "decamped", Almost eaquealing the exploits of Gov. [Wilson] Shanon.[36] If you will push the buisiness you are in for a year and a half, you may have a thousand clear, put that into cattle sheep and colts, you can soon draw from it what will improve a quarter [section] of Land for which you can have a deed any day. In this way you can open a richer "Gold placer", than exists at "Pikes Peak, or in California", With this advantage that there is no risk about it. Your hea[l]th, morrals, and industrious habits are not endangered, and you are not thrown into close association with drunkards vagabons, gamblers, robers, and cut throats.

All that are going from here are reckless Any of them when removed from restraint if unsuccessful would [be] ready to become highwaymen Brewer 3 of the Ellises, and a brotherinlaw, James Hartman and a number of others of the same class. But tho I have written all this I trust you will not hastily make such a move. If you do whatever our regrets we will try to be reconciled as every one must act according to their own reason and judgement, This life is realy of no consequence but as it fixes and developes some character or quality good or evil which quality will be the measure of our happiness, or misery.

If you can raise me two hundred dollars from Mr. O[sborne] I will get through as best I can, by geting time from [William B.] Daniels and Co, and on what I owe Woodbury till I can get the Land sold.[37] If Mr O[sborne] gets the money he looks for I would be glad to get one thousand till I can make the sale.

In some respects I would like to go to Georgia very much. I would like a warmer climate I think too I should like Mr O[sborne] not that I expect I could agree with him in every thing. I do not expect that in any one, But I admire the

generous disposition he manifests,   it is worth more than
gold to have a friend fired by noble ends. Errors of the head
in such men are of small account, and easily overlooked particularly if we allow ourselves to reflect on our own   But the
more I reflect the less I think it possible that I can leave here.
If I cannot an effort must be made to have better families
come in and buy out the miserable set that are here   those
who stay will in that case improve

   We have received papers to the 12th inst. The winter is
called mild tho to me it is cold

   All send their love

Your affectionate father
J. H. Williams

If it is possible do not fail to send me two hundred dollars, till
I can get my feet under me   If the amount cannot be raised
at once send it at different times as indicated in my letter to
Mr. O[sborne]

From J. H. Williams

Homer Hamilton Co.
March 3 1859

Dear James

   I am sitting down to write to you from habit rather than
from any thing important, I have to communicate. No
Letters or papers since I wrote to you

   On the evening of the first, a dry snow commenced falling
and continued all night, and till after mid day yesterday—
There was more wind and it was altogether the worst storm
of the winter   It was not so cold, but as the weather had
been very fine . . . some trifling exceptions for some time previous, it was felt to be quite cold. The drifts are larger than
any before this winter,   For some ten or 12 hours, the snow
"Keltered", after the style of [18]56−7.   Tho the snow fell
dry at one time on the morning of the 2nd it indicated rain.

There was some lightning, indicating a heavy rain south of us, and were it not for the drifting I prefer the snow decidedly— Were I to go south I would want to go further south than our old position in Ohio. A latitude like that of Texas, Tenesee, or Ga, must have many advantages could an equeally productive soil be obtained. I have never lived however farther south than southeastern [Ohio] and cannot therefore weigh properly, the disadvantages of a southern climate. I doubt whether it is possible for the *earth* to be so productive where the winters are short, particularly where the frosts are light. It seems to be a principle of *Divine Order* that most subjects in order to develope their intrinsic excellence must be submitted to a course of severe discipline. Those things of which it may be said, that strictly speakeing, they do not have their to pass through the "furnace of affliction, or trial", Still before their use appears they do pass through some thing analogus there to. The Gold must be "tried in the fire" before it is pronounced, "virgin", The vine when taken too far south must have its rest from the exercise of vegitative life, its time of *torture* or *trial*. As winter does not bring this about, it is effected by removeing the earth & sourses of nutriment from its roots, When these are returned, and its "sufferings are ended" it is again productive. The food taken into the stomach must be submitted to a series of *castigations*, flagilations, or in the Language of physiologists, it must be severly "Tortured", before the nutricious, and in nutricious matters can be seperated, and rendered fit to support the animal econemy. Were we to pass our lives in sunshine, and prosperity— Had we no "losses nor crosses" internal nor external the real gold could not be made to apper— nor could we be persuaded, much less could we be led to reflect long enoug[h], to *see* and *beleive*, that evil and selfish affections had a real root in us; and that to be happy they must be irradicated, and oposite ones be implanted in their stead. Those who cannot be benefited by these trials that is, who cannot be regenerated are not in the Divine providence permited to come into *them* Those of an internal order but have in their stead, worldy cares, trials, losses, and vexations, which to a

certain extent humble, restrain, and as it were keep them in
bonds and thus modify their *characters* & *evils* The word is
full of the discription of the various forms of those trials and
their uses to us in fitting us for eternal happiness by building
up the Lords-kingdom within us. The *harsh winter frosts*,
winds, and *snows*, do all for the earth which spiritual winter
and times of trial do for us. They open and seperate those
substances too glutinously, and tenaciously combined The
earth itself is opened, and pulverized, and so fretted that it
readily gives forth its own nutriciouse gasses to the open
mouths of the hungry plants, and in return for all it gives
up, receives rich supplies from the snows rains and the at-
mosphere. It is because the sources just indicated are inex-
austible that inteligent cultivation improves the productive
capacity of the soil, while ignorant and negligent cultivation
always exhaust it. These are but hints of some of the things
which lead me to think that a northern climate, soil being eaqueal, is prefferable. Of course there is a limit, and if the idea
be correct, the question is what degree of Latitude and Al-
titude would be the best

When I look at some of the advantages of a southern Latitude, that of Ga. for instance, and compare it with ours, it
seems that while we are spending more than half our time in
"batling the elements", the inhabitants of Ga unmolested by
cold, or the terror of it, are attending to buisiness. The necessity for *Warm Ho[u]ses*, warm *clothing* and large amounts of
Fuel require much more effort in the north than in the south.
But if it be true, that health is better in the north, that as already hinted winter in her severest forms, has its use. That
the earth is more productive after the visits of *harsh frosts*.
That a northern climate invigorates both physically and men-
tally, while southern Tempreture relaxes both If all be true
then the disadvantages of a northern position are more than
compensated by the advantages

No news from Ohio. School interest conti[n]ues, with
our usual routine of duties and labors. Have not yet decided
whether I shall have any farming done or not. With the boys
in school it will not be profitable for me to have much done

in that way beyond the Town Lots and should I be able to move in the fall (by disposing of the Town property for something I could take along or have) and conclude to do so it would be a disadvantage to put forth a farming effort this spring and summer. Besides it is not required as I will be buisy enough without it.

Do not undertake to write too often   it will either be too hard on you, or interfere with your attention to matters of more importance, and when you do write (tho I confess I am much gratified with the various information you give) we will all be pleased with a short letter

Remember me kindly to Mr O[sborne]. All send their love.

Ma is going to make an effort to write soon

Your affectionate father

J. H. Williams

From J. H. Williams

Homer Hamilton Co Iowa

March 28 1859

Dear James

Three letters have been rec'd since my last. Your last is dated [March] 13th inst. One of them without date evidently the middle one. A number of [news]papers have come lately. we are all glad to hear from you so often. The pleasure of hearing from you, has taken the place of that of seeing you. We are so constituded that one pleasure readily takes the place of an other. The papers too, are quite an item in the sources of our gratifications. Through them we are becoming acquainted with, and acquireing an interest in southern, and particularly in *Georgia–affairs*   Always bating [reading with anticipation] the *shooting*, and affrays so frequently reported

I think that we would all like the Climate of *Ga.* The summer bloom you are enjoying, must be cheering indeed, when compared with the *sombre gloom* that still hangs over the vegitable world in our northern climate. We have had what is called here, a mild and pleasant winter, but it was terriffic when compared with the one you are passing (I should say have passed through) for you are entering upon what would constitute our summer.

I am glad you continue to report the weather & Tempreture. It enables me to judge of Matters that I have always felt a deep interest in. . . .

Our stock has increased to 54 head.   14 of them cows & heffers   5 calves have come this spring and as they are well fed, they are fine fellows; it would do you good to see them play—   expect 6 or 7 more this summer from present stock— Think will have 100 head or over if nothing occurs to prevent by fall. With money could soon have more than that   I pay 10 to 15$ for Cows—   Trade goods, flour, and groceries, and collect some debt in that way—   If I could get [a]round, might *perhaps* collect more,   Some will never pay in any way, as they do not intend it

The P[ikes] P[eak] fever is as high in certain quarters here as ever. There is nothing certain however about it. There is doubtless gold there, but there are evidently more persons interested in geting up *Town plots and selling lots*, in supplying provisions at enormous rates, in Tavern cities, in Steam Boat and stage lines, than in the "*gold digings*", to say nothing of the hosts of *Black-legs*, *Theives*, and *Land pirates*, who with all their might fan the flame in the hope of fleeceing the verdant; or in some way profiting by the excitement.   Flour has risen there to 30$ per sack. Some, who have returned, say they have not tasted bread for 3 months—   That there is gold, but that it will not pay—   many working hard and not makeing fifty cents a day. Others report profits large, but give such bewildered accounts, that their statements are unreliable. If the best accounts, *be true*, those who are successful there, will perform a use—   That of the "*Long eared quadrupid*," [mule] who *carries patiently* the *Treasure*, to *those who actively persue* their *regular*, and *proper* callings.

We have got our Teacher employed for a spring and summer session of 4 months,   will end in July— and will make 8 months in succession   The children all go,   Rebecca stands in well. We are all very buisy   Mother and I attend to everything–   They are as much engaged evenings and Mornings as in school   This, I mean the school, has removed the greatist source of uneasiness we had, and could I sell the O[hio] property so as to pay off and get even a small surplus to work on, we at times think we would be as happy here as any where– particularly so, if once fairly embarked in the stock business. In that case, we imagine you here, with a small capital, *in* it, which with care would soon grow larger, and support you hansomely; without the confinement of a Watch *bench*– or *Store*– or *Counting-Room*–   True, close, and constant attention would have to be given,   There can be no success without zealous effort always, and at time, *indomitable courage*, and energy must be *exerted*; or the most feasible and useful enterprise will utterly fail! Where these reveries flit through my mind, I fancy Mother and myself occasionally, And you and the boys, frequently takeing the *girls* out in buisiness excursions, so that having got a good education, the[y] may see, and Know the world, and become weomen of "Sense," not ready to marry any gassing fool, that may cross their path

No better can be expected if they are cooped up in such society as this. This very evening *Mary Hartman* who is living at Mr Walkers has invited Bella to a party. She has managed Mrs. W. to Let her have one. She is cracked about the Teacher. She will have him and Columbus Pemberton and has invited Bella! What is to be done? Just think of it! It explains the whole subject I am driving at. If in the present "Infernal state of society", Arristocracy has its evils, this *arogant sensless Mobacracy*, has them of no less magnitude. Bella is at school,   when she comes we will leave it to herself   she acts pretty promptly and decidely in such cases. We think she will decline the honor and save us the hostility it would excite were we to do it.

I hope Mr O[sborne] may succeed in geting his affairs into an easy state. Whether I succeed in going south or not. I may say that I hope it for his sake, for your sake– and I may add for my own sake. He is a generous minded man and it does one good to see such successful. I do not mean by this that he or any one here below need be expected to be perfect, To Err is "human", to be good is angelic & to be goodness itself is Divine. We are informed, by the writings of the church that the Angels take great delight in their various employments, but that an "inkling of glory" can be detected in it— They are not the most perfect— Yet they are angels, We can well afford then, to excuse a considerable amount of it, in those who like ourselves are yet in this Rudimental state; the work of regeneration but imperfectly operative in some things— commenceing, in regard to others not yet commenced, because not yet discovered to be evils. The discovery of evil must preceed refformation. Still more, must it preceed *regeneration*. All who interiorly acknowledge the *Lord*, will in due time be given to see their evils, and be enabled to put them away. The Divine Love secures and effects this. If evils are not seen, and in freedom put away, the end which is human happiness, is frustrated. This work of discovery and purgation in its commencement is refformation. In its fulness it is regeneration The man is made new— Is *born again*— becomes a celestial Angel which is but an other name for *wisdom* and goodness in form. Such attend little do not atall attend to appearances, not even to incidental or evanescent motives, but to the ruleing ends which are constant, and to which every thing else is sub-servient. These *ruling ends*, they perceive at once— and excuse, or condemn him whom the end excuses or condems. But in the mixed state of good and evil, which pervails here, We have to do altogether with acts— *still with motives* in acts, but judged by acts— not by a single one but by the tenor of them— Thus if a mans acts are upon the whole bad, we should say properly if his motives are like his acts he is a bad man. And we ought to avoid him, but good Mens weakness and foibles should be very leniently dealt with. The scriptures agree with the writings of the church, where they declare that the "Heavens are not clean before him". Men then, may have foibles, when the Angels have them, We have them, and by them through the *good* and the *true* we receive

from him the Lord   he leads us to heaven if we will but follow. Or more correctly, he leads by *truths*, and *goods* from
himself to *himself*, and bends our falicies and evils, if we will
suffer it, so that they do not obstruct or hinder the Kingdom
of god being formed within. I dwell on these themes because
I believe them to be *real*, and natural things to be unreal except so far as they are subservient to spiritual things—   then
they are real   then it is, that the Ea[r]th becomes the foundation of the *Heavens*!

I am glad you will not have to sit so close. I always feard
to have you do it,   I am glad to think too, that you are active and attentive from principle. And that you have no
associates,   you do not need them. Now is the time, to
form buisiness habbits, and a correct judgement of men and
things. Those who suffer fools and Knaves at your age, to
intrude on their time, and attention will *never* be *wise*. Conduct yourself on the 3 *fold principle* of strict *morrality— Honesty*, and Relegion, which means the *Supreme Love* of *God*,
and you will never lack inward consolation, nor the confidence and esteem of the wise and the good.

I have no more light on the O[hio] affairs. I need not say to
do what you can for me. I know you will as soon as you can.
Can say nothing more about what I will, or can do at present. Mother and all fine in sending their love   Remember me
to Mr O[sborne]

Your affectionate father
J. H. Williams

From J. H. Williams

Homer Hamilton Co Iowa
April 17 1859

Dear James

Letters and papers till 27th ult are received   no more
news from Ohio. I fear a long delay before a sale can be effected, which will ware out the patience of Messurs Wood-

bury and W B Daniels and Co. I have paid off all other claims here. The small ones annoyed me so much, that I applied two hundred dollars out of the proceeds of Mr Woodburys flour to do it. Which with the old claim will make 450$. If Mr O[sborne] can do no more, I hope he will enable you to send me $200, immediately. If I pay that I think he will not trouble me about the old 250$ till I make the sale. I have not been sued for any thing yet, but it is *terrible torture* to be anxious to pay, the time past in which it should be done, and to be able to do so little!

I will be very glad to have you continue your observations on the tempreture and the weather. I begin to feel as much desire to know the peculiarities of a Ga *spring*, and *summer* as I do those of the winter

We have severe winter yet. This month has been very rough, and cold. Three snowstorms in this month, and freezeing that would do credit to Jan[uary] even in this latitude. The winter had been called a beautiful one, but all admit now that it has been tedious, and severe. It commenced 9th of Nov.   Stock are suffering from want of food as usual I am selling hay. Were it not for the scarcity of money I would sell quite as much as would pay for the Cuting. As it is shall sell over 40$ worth.

I would like to know what you think of a southern climate particuarly that of Ga during the Spring and summer months. Are you troubled with insects of any kind? Will not the summer months be enervateing to northern constitutions? Are pulmonary affections common? I will be glad of all the information on these points your position may enable you to obtain. We may reasonably expect the same Latitude to be characterized by the same phenomina generally, modified by difference of soil, and local circumstances. There are many things that we like here   it is destined to be a fine country, but we begin to think that there are too many difficulties to contend with, and that in particular we would prefer shorter and lighter winters; if eaqueal advantages in regard to health, and fertility of soil could be obtained.

The fever for Pikes Peak continues as fervid as ever, tho

the reports from there are varied and contradictory. There may be gold, but as in the case of California when the first rush took place Ninety nine out of the 100 will make nothing by diging! Money will be made, but it is done in other ways. For a while every thing is very high in new countries till the reaction takes place which must happen sooner or later. It is unsafe in such a state to do any buisiness. The reason money is plenty under such circumstances, (at first) is, it is carried there and is freely spent for necessaries at high rates   This state of things may last for sometime when the inundation of population is caused by a gold excitement, and that excitement has some real foundation to rest on. "Shrewed ones", Make fortunes in such cases. Some do it honestly, but for the most part it is done by preying on the "verdancy", of those who bring in money, or property, or who by hard labor earn it in the mines. But while it is entirely over looked, by the excited I might add ignorant beings that are runing a way from this state, in quest of Gold; there is more gold, in the green carpet which covers these extended plains, than can be obtained from any mine in California, or Pikes P., were the same capital energy and skill invested in Sheep, that must be put into requisition to dig gold successfully. $50 000 000 was produced in California last year, but there is no rush there now. Indeed it is well known that there is a great deal of suffering there $50 000 000 looks large on paper, but it is really nothing in comparison with the value of the products of a thriveing in state about which there [is] little or nothing said; and it would go but a little way in purchasing the comforts enjoyed by Massachusetts, New York, Pensylvania, Ohio, or Ga. Callifornia will no doubt make a fine state not so much because there is *Gold*, there as because a large portion of it is well suited to agriculture, and manufactures may be successfully prosecuted   But her importance as a state must remain relatively insignificant till mechanical agricutural and manufacturing industry gets at least eaqueal attention to her gold mines. Till then there will be more gold in Boston, New York, London, or Parris than in Sanfrancisco and can be obtained on better terms at these points   The reason is obvious. They produce those values in abundance which gold only represents. *"But a truce"*. I know you are not going on a *"wild-goose chase"* of gold hunting, and I am filling my sheet with matter about which I intended to say but a word or two. But the subject is exciting so much attention that it is as eligible as any other for remark

The interest continues in the school and Ma's Labors and mine are constant of course to keep matters straight and prevent interruption. Indeed it is the only thing we take interest in

There is still some work to do notwithstanding the stringency of money

I have had, and settled off another account, with Mr. Walker. That $7 of the newhouse ac[coun]t. I have not settled. Your letter to N[ewhouse] was never answered, which silence, as he said he had returned all Mr W[alker]'s account amounts to a denial of it. I told Mr. W[alker] I would write to him. I want you therefore to give me his address. Mr. W[alker] was disposed to denie that he had written off an account to you, with that item thrown out, I have seen it but I believe I misslaid it. I suppose if newhouse will not pay it, or cannot be found, I must loose it, tho I think it likely from his manner of doing buisiness that he paid it. Mr W[alker] admits he did pay him money more than once

Remember me to Mr
O[sborne]
Your affectionate father
J. H. Williams

From Eleanor & J. H. Williams

Homer Aprile 29 1859

Dear James,

If any one had told me when you left that I would let so long a time pass without writing. I would not have believed

it possible, but Pa was writeing often and it seemed little difference which wrote, indeed I have exerted myself beyond my strength to keep the children at school but we feel amply paid in the advancement they have made. John and Bella will be through the Arithmetic this term they commenced at the beginning and cought up with the first class, passed them and are now in advance; and have progressed equally well in their other studies. We have a most excellent teacher we consider this the best school they have ever attended and look upon it as providential that we have been able to procure him. I believe the children have learned more than they would have done at Urbanna [Ohio] or any other place[38] we have no company or any excitements to divert their attention from their studies

There is a constant emigration from the north to Pikes Peak and Washington Teritory some are returning. Our town is being improved by takeing away the old houses two were taken to Ft Dodge on the snow

You speak of flowers if Bella could see them she would be delighted she brought in a wild crocus the other day that had been hardy enough to brave the cold winds, but we have very little grass yet. Pa and I have had many long talks during this long and tedious spring about what we had better do and sometimes wish that our lot had been cast in a warmer clime, but now that the weather is pleasant and we see the farmers at work on our rich soil, with the prospect of an abundant harvest we think perhaps we have our share of comforts and instead of complaining we should endeavor to be more thankful for our many blessings. I have serious doubts whether my constitution would bear the relaxation of a southern summer. I want you to tell us what you think about it

You know pa always gets discouraged when he thinks he is of no use in the [Swedenborgian] Church, and the prospects here do not brighten. he talks some of takeing a trip this fall through southern Illinois and Tennesse and see if we cannot locate ourselves better in that respect. the church is in the

wilderness and her people are scattered.   if there is a use for
us to perform there will be an opening.

One thing is certain   this is destined to be a great country
at no very distant period,   we have already heard the shrill
whistle of the steam king at our door,   a [steam]boat has
made its third trip up to Ft Dodge this spring[39]

The boys have gone out to the [farm on the] section to day
to bring in their tools and prepare for working the lots in
town   John has taken his rifle with the hope of getting some
game   Bella and Rebecca are fixing a bed at the south side
of the house to plant the Cotton seeds you sent them   I wish
you could see how well Rebecca looks   she runs about on the
prairie just as she used to do but is a very little stooped
John is getting worse every day.   he is well in health. I wonder if shoulder braces would do him any good

If thought made presence you would have frequent visitors   there does not a day pass that we do not think and talk
of you   when I lie down at night I think of you in your little
room and pray that the Lord will guide and direct you.
though we miss you very much it was better for you not to be
here this winter   we have no society[,] hard times, and little
to do in the way of business.

I am glad you have turned over that new leaf   it will be
much more conducive to your health to make such a disposition of your time; as the heat increases be cautious about
takeing too long walks

Columbus has been attending the lectures in Keokuk this
winter and is gone now to Swede Point to practice[40]   he is
not well since he came home   the whole family looks broken
down

There are some changes among the you[n]g people   Adelia Moore is married to Mr McFetters and Menerve DeWitt
to a Mr Shaw that lost his wife some three months ago

Bella received the book you sent her but was pursueing
her studies with so much ardor that she would not read it
until vacation   the term was out last friday. John did not
have so much self denial and got some black marks in con-

sequence   I have read part of it and like it next to Davie
Copperfield
   They have returned from the place   well pleased as usual
pa thinks it looks so beautiful and the boys [are] excited with
their success in shooting a crane   wishing you were here to
get some of it

                         Much love from all
                         Your Mother
                         E. F. Williams

Dear James
   I will add to what ma has told you, that we have no news
yet from Ohio. Do not intend to have much farming done,
think we will plant nothing but the Lots— in corn and vegetables generally. But that will [be] quite a little farm as we
have about 4 acres fenced. The last impropitious season has
made this a very scarce year here, tho prices do not rule so
high as I feared, owing doubtless to the scarcity of money.
   When the children get tired with out door work and the
open air you will hear from them all. The [school] session
lasted 6 months—   They have 4 weeks vac[a]tion which will
be followed by a two month session   After an other short vacation we hope to have the school continued

                         affectionately yours
                         J. H. Williams

From J. H. Williams

                         Homer Hamilton Co Iowa
                         May 15 1859
Dear James
   Your Letters to 17 of April are received. The Spring
opened beautifully with the first of May, and we soon began
to think little of the tediousness of the winter   the last two or
three days is disposed to be wet and somewhat colder. We

have nothing new. The children have this month as a vacation   we are planting our lots to amount of about 4 acres
which is probaly all the farming we'll attempt this year.

The Land scape wares the same enchanting aspect which
it always assumes in the summer, tho we think it more beautiful this spring than ever before. There seems to be nothing
to regret but the absence of congenial friends and acquaintances. If debts were paid off the scarcity of money is not to be
regretted,   it will do good by correcting many vices, and it
will soon come in when active industry is pushed.

I got a letter from Grand Pa [Anderson] a few days ago
could tell nothing then when the Long buisiness could be
closed as court was in session and Cowen had not been to see
him at the time he wrote

Grand Pa gives a gloomy picture of the state of things in
Belmont [County, Ohio],   at least 8 convicts would be sent
to the penetentiary, and one or two Murder cases. He as-
scribes it to demagogueism in pushing schools causeing men
to hate work This is the appearance but not the truth. It is
true that to cultivate the Intellect, and neglect the affections,
or the head, without the heart, leades to *schemeing, idleness*
and *crime*. It prepares a man to be a "greater" devil   But the
true cause, is to be found, in the cause, which leads to such
mode of education   Why are the *loves*, the sources of mans
actions neglected? It is because it is beleived, from the teaching which has been and still is, to a great extent general that
mans acts do not condemn him, but his faith. This leads to
cultivating the understanding only. Evil works are not shuned
but concealed, and the source from which they flow remains
impure. Let the church teach that evils must be *shuned* as
sins against God, that works condemn and not faith! Then
the more a man is educated the better he will be. He will
not look on education then as the means of seting him above
others, thus inflateing his *pride* and makeing a *Demon* of
him   but he will look upon it as the means of being useful—
fiting him properly to discharge the functions of some useful
employment. The cause then of the fearful increase of crime
and dishonesty every where is not to be attibuted to educa-

tion! But to *Justification* by *faith alone* Remember me to Mr
O[sborne]
your affectionate father
J. H. Williams

From Eleanor Williams

Homer May 29 .59
Dear James
Yours of the fifteenth was received gladly as we had been
looking for some days, also one of the thirteenth for pa, containing draft for $100, which pa is very thankful for, and
thinks if he had as much more he could get along until the
land in Ohio is sold, we have not heard anything in regard
to it since pa ordered it to be sold
We have nothing new the weather is pleasant but rather
cool. I want to know if the heat of your summer is not as
hard to bear as the cold of our winter and if the stock thrive
as well as they do with us
It gives us much pleasure to know you are well and contented, you have reason to be thankful for a position in
which you can make a comfortable living in an honorable
way
We are unsuited to pioneering and a change would seem
desireable but we must remain we can see no possibility of
being able to leave, pa has fenced the lot south of us in with
the garden and sowed the yard in grass, all the trees in the
garden are growing finely one is full of cheries, those on
the square are not so flourishing except whot are in your corner There are no [religious] meetings now last sabath we
walked on the prairie. though we often lament the want of
society I could not help thinking it was much better for the
children to be surrounded by the works of the divine hand
than to be in the false and corrupt society of this day,
Your ideas on slavery sounds rather odd. it is doubtless
very agreeable to the master to be relieved from all the severe

labor, but is it agreeable to the slave to perform it?   is it liveing by the golden rule which says do to others as you would
have others do to you

Where they are well cared for they have less care than they
would if they provided for themselves.   still it puts it in the
power of cruel and imprincipled masters to abuse and opress
them.   however, it speaks well for the sistem when a risi-
dence in the south generally dispells these scruples.[41]

Pa and the children are all out planting.   it is harvest with
you before we begin to plant.   it certainly must take less la-
bour to live in such a climate

Mr Hartman and a number of others after stakeing their all
to go to P[ikes] P[eak] are returning

All go in love to you

E. Williams

From Bella Williams

Homer Hamilton Co. Iowa
June 6 1859

Dear James

It is along time since I received your letter but it kept me
busy in school and out of it to keep up with my class so I put
off answering your letter until vacation. Since then I have
thought every day that I would write.   but we have been so
busy that I never felt that I had time.

Pa got the vacation continued a week longer than was intended in order to get the planting and other work done before the commencement of school. Mr. Blair returned a fort
night ago, and the vacation is now ended   school will take
up tomorrow.

I planted some of the cotton seeds (you sent me) about five
weeks ago.   four of which came up, but on the twenty fifth
of May, it rained and blew very hard all day and the previous
night. On the evening of the twenty fifth it cleared up cold. I
neglected to cover my cotton plants and the consequence was

they were killed by the frost. Nothing els was as injured I have planted some since but I am afraid they will be to late.

Ma Pa Rebecca George and I took a long walk on the prairie Sunday before last   the day was very fine, and the prairie looked so green and pretty with here and there a herd of cattle grazing, that I longed for you to be with us.

Last Thursday we all (except Pa) went in the ox wagon to Curriers Mill to fish. When we started the wind was blowing quite cold on the prairie, but when we reached the timber we did not feel it at all. We could not go quite to the [Boone] river with the wagon on account of some timber haveing fallen across the road; so we had to get out and walk about three quarters of a mile, and in crossing prairie creek had the misfortune to slip off the foot log into the water but soon got out with out any more damage than wet feet. As soon as we reached the river we made preparations for fishing by untiing our fishing poles. I caught three before the rest felt a bite;   we fished for several hours but only caught ten.

Mrs Walker has a Melodeon which Mr. Walker bough[t] of Mr Church for one hundred dollars. Mr Church had bought it from a family at Spirit Lake who were going to Pikes Peak. I went over to Mr Walkers yesterday to try it. It is of Mahogany and is of a some what different shape but very little larger than ours.   the keys were very much swollen with the damp weather   were so stiff that it was almost impossible to play upon them. I think it arrived here from Spirit Lake day before yesterday.[42]

I have been trying during vacation to learn some of the music you sent me. I am learning "Fishers Hornpipe" and "The Willow song". I like the latter very much. I believe you used to play them both.   did you not?

We had a few vegetables from the garden last week for the first time this season.

I hope you will find no bad spelling in this short letter. We all send our love to you.

From your affectionate sister,
Bella

From J. H. Williams

Homer Hamilton Co Iowa   July 11 1859

Dear James

Your letter to Ma is the last rec'd   as soon as she can she will write. She has not been so well this spring and summer— but is better now—   I attribute it to having too much to do to keep all in order for school.

The year since you left is nearly through   it has been a year of difficulty as was to be expected owing to the wet and failure of crops for two years previous and the improvident Character of the people. The difficulties have not been so great however as I feared they would be. Prices of provisions are lower than was to have been expected, the *entire scarcity or want* of *money*, has kept them down. Now that the new crops are coming in (all which look well) and releif is here, it is a matter of *astonishment how many have got a long*

No news when the ohio affair will be brought to a close. First of August is almost here, and I can make no arrangement for Mr. Beyler. It would therefore ease my mind very much, if it were possible for you to send a draft To Mortimore Pollock Clarington Monroe Co O[hio] for fifty dollars. I have got him to attend to it. It will save 15 or 20 days to send it to him direct. Of course Mr O[sborne]'s circumstance, and your own, must be consulted in the Matter, And let me get along as best I can,   But as I see the "*panic*" is passing away in the south, I hope Mr O[sborne] will find the firm footing in his buisiness, his energy and perserverence deserves.

Iowa never looked more delightful and promiseing. All that is wanting is *capital, industry, true Christianity* or morral worth in the people, to make it a very "paradise." If the attention of a few good and true men were turned this way, I would not think of leaving it. As it is, I am in a great strait about what to do   The stock is doing finely, 61 head   12 this spring   Calves, some of them 4 or 5 months old, are larger than last years stock, 14 to 15 months old. The weather is quite warm, as much so as is compatable with the good of stock. The bight of the winter inclines me to the south but the heat of summer, and other difficulties attendent on a southern Climate, quite compensates the matter and leads me to beleive this the most happily bal[ance]d position after all! The soil is so productive that abundant supplies for the winter are easily raised   I see too, that the climate is as capricious in the *south*, and *east*, (north with you) as in the west, and this season much more so,   *South* & *Southwest*, as in Texas to secure crops, early planting becomes necessary; which exposes the crop to the effect of capricious change of tempreture, as much as in this climate. For this reason Ohio, and southern Ill[inois] is not as certain for fruit as it will be here where vegitation has a longer "*and more even sleep.*"

I told you that for the purpose of lessening chores, and so as to attend more readily to those which were unavoidable, I brought my work last fall to the house. I left the jewelry and most of the common watches in the Trunk in the storeroom, as there was no sale for them. I ceased to value them and was too careless,   For a time the boys slept in the room but this was troublesome, and was dropt. The consequence was that some villian took charge of all the good articles including the package of broken Bank bills that was in a Tin box Hen[ry] D[a]lly is suspected and is closely watched by several   In one instance he offered west[ern] union paper a pacage of which was in the lot[43]

Write as often as convenient   a short note is all you might to tax yourself with
Remember me to Mr. O[sborne]

Your affectionate father
J. H. Williams

From J. H. & George Williams

Homer Hamilton Co Iowa 1859 July 24
Dear James
As the mail will close in a few minutes I have but time to say that Cowen has failed to close my business so as to meet

the claim of Beyler. It amounts [to] 60.33   I have just enclosed the bal[ance] to Mortimore Pollock and have to depend on you for the 50$. If it is not yet started I will be glad
[if] you could have it done as soon as possible As there is no
telling when Cowen will be able to close the buisiness. I will
be very glad to get the bal. of the 100$ I can then fight the
battle pretty well

Mr Pollock is so anxious Beyler should have his money
that he would pay it but their buisiness has been disasterous
for a year and they are embarrassed. He knows that my re-
liance is on the sale of the Land by Cowen   I have informed
in this letter that I cannot get it from that source, and that
it will be sent by you. I have also requested him to pay it on
the first– that a draft from you of fifty will soon be received

I am really harder run to manage the few hundred dollars
I now owe than I was to arrange 40 000$ in [18]37–40
and 41. But thanks to the Divine Providence I am nearly
through   50$ After the payment now makeing will enable
me to hold all still till the Land is sold

I am still collecting claims in stock. I begin to think it will
number 100 head this fall   If the Land is not sold within six
or eight months, I will drive the stock east and sell and pay
off. I dislike to do this however as the largest portion is
young and increaseing rapidly in value   The season continues beautiful   Tho John is in school He captures as many
as 6 to 11 chicks in a day   Rolf is as good and keen as ever.

Your affectionate father
J. H. Williams

You need not hurry yourself or Mr O[sborne] about the 2nd
Fifty Dollars   I can keep things still a little while yet

One thing I forgot to mention   You are aware that we
have had a good Teacher   He has left for Webster City
where he has p[r]operty and is married. With a little attention you could soon qualify your self to teach and can board
at home and get 35$ per month spending 6 hours in the day
and 5 days in the week   The pay is public money

I know there will be no objection in the board of Education. I am President of the board. But whether you would like this or not, there will be enough for you to do, and I am pe[r]suaded it will tell better, than what you are doing (if your wages are not raised)   To say nothing of the advantages of the freedom it will give you, and the pleasure it will be to us all to have you at home. School will open first Nov. and will hold 10 months in the year with 2 months vacation

J. H. Williams

Since writing I have had a dunar [debt collector]   This makes me break through my resolution to wory you no more about money

There is no information yet as to when Cowen can bring my affair in ohio to a close. The 50$ I borrowed of Beyler I have got notice that he wants first of August. I have no reliable way to raise it, tho I must promise to do so some way. If you can send me 100$ more before that time it will greately releive me,   If you can, send 50$ checks   it will be more convenient, as division can not be effected here

We think a good deal about Texas. Tho we are not sure that frontier life anywhere, will suit us. But a move now, would ruin us altogether. The property in O[hio] will go for little, in consequence of the presure which continues there but it must go to settle these debts. I could in the case of removal get nothing for Town property & household goods which I could not take a long. You see the difficulties to be contended with

On the other hand I am makeing expenses at my buisiness— Stock is improveing and increasing   Cattle now number 57 head 6 of them Old Oxen. Had I killed them as I tho't some of doing last fall when fat I would have made my money out of the beef this summer. They look fine and will do something with them this fall

We expect to raise something handsome towards our support off the Lots so that if out of debt we could live so far as comforts are concerned very well

But so far as social enjoyment are concerned we have none but what we instinctively avoid. Writing to you and looking for and reading your letters & the few papers we take & those you send constitu[t]e the sum of our sources of gratification except what arrives from the conciousness of an effort to do our duty

J. H. Williams

If you can not send two— 50$ checks so that I could forward one of them to O[hio] before the first [of] August so s[end] me one if p[ossible] I know this is annoying   I hope soon to be able to avoid it. If there was any effort or turn I could make it would gladly be done

I enclose you Georges letter in this. I send it as it is,   he is very sensative about it. He has labored hard on it.

Thinking you could not read it and fearing he will be discouraged we do not set Him to write it again   I am afraid we have put Parke[r] back amonth seting him to write over again.   he is doing all he can to learn A[nd] had a letter ready sometime ago

Copy

Dear James

I would like to see you very much. Rolf is geting fine   we let him lie in the Kitchen. I took Rebecca up to Mr Clarkes They live in part of Mr Churches house. Sule Clark calculates to get a pair of Boots when she gets above me in my class. But I do not intend to let her   Remember me to Mr O[sborne]   he will hear from me soon

George Hite

I like the idea of the mastic roofing but fear that the canvas in the foundation will prevent duribility

We are up in the morning by daylight   Ma as a general thing an hour first. It is a hurry to let the children get to school   I cut the most of the Wood, Milk, & feed,   Finding it impossible to manage all, and attend at the store and keep up prices there   I have moved my bench, and the articles most wanted to the house. When I get warmed & have a spare moment the room is in order, I can go to work and hard as matters are, It is accounting to a good deal. We are geting our wood hauled by those who can not pay otherwise what they owe.

The Pianno stands along the west wall   My bench is in the N[orth] West cor[ner], and a Box with a lot of goods on it stands at the right hand of the door as you enter. The kitchen being sealed the boys bed is in the end of it (south) The Pump house receives the wood and all the things that clutter the house. I traded for a common carpet for the front room   Our quarters you see are very close. Still as a whole as we set the table in the kitchen We are more comfortable than we have been in Iowa

[J. H. Williams]

TWO

Stock farms cannot fail to be a good buisiness here.
—J. H. Williams

"Lessons of humility and of humanity"

From J. H. Williams

Homer Hamilton Co Iowa Aug 28 1859

Dear James

I cannot but feel deep regret that under the circumstances you have engaged to stay away so long as an other year.   to be so closely confined for all you can save   Look at this year. Your saving after deducting expense of trip out and back, is less than 100$. Hard as the times are, had your mind been made up to it, you could in various ways have made and saved more here. More would have been mad[e] by collecting my ac[coun]ts lost, or in the way of beeing lost for want of attention, which I cannot give them as the children must go to school making such demands on my time that it is impossible for me to do anything with those who do not call on me for settlement— Still I think Your acc[oun]t has been useful,   every young man (there may be exceptions) should have one. It "unmasks" the world to him. It is not then to be regretted viewed in that light. . . .

I got a letter lately from Cowen in which he says he will get a decree in this month and can offer the Land for sale in oct.   Should a sale be effected it will be better for you to be here, should there be but 3 to 500$ after settling liabilities. With that *sum*, the stock clear, the Land, and our houses, which can all be brought into use, by putting them on the

Land, and what can yet be gathered out of the accounts, a
good start can be made, and without confinement   if you
should relish the buisiness, more can be allowed you than it is
possible for you to save where you are at the end of the year.
The stock now numbers 66 head and is worth 11 to 1200$
most of it growing rapidly in value   There will however be
more than five hundred dollars left from the sale or I shall be
sadly disappointed
   Do what you think best and May the Lord direct which if
you trustingly look to him he will do.

Your affectionate father

J. H. Williams

From Eleanor Williams

                                    Tuesday morning Sep 28 1859
Dear James
   We received yours in answer to pa and are glad you have
decided as you have,   it is better for the present though we
feel as we did not like to have you away any longer.   but we
must try to put away selfishness and do what is for the best
   They are still working at the hay and have some eighty
tuns   pa has been so busy and so tired he could not write. I
have never thanked you for the pleasure you have given me in
the reading of [Charlotte Bronte's] Jane Eyre   It was quite
a surprise to me   it was so very different from what I had
imagined a girl of her experience and knowledge of the world
could write.   the caracters connected with the school are
doubtless taken from life and she shows them up beautifully,   but her hero I do not like and how a young girl
like her could get up such a caracter is a mystery, but it is
[Charles] Dickens that makes his caracters live and move
this story of [Dickens'] Domby and Son is next to Davy
Copperfield in my estimation
   I had intended to write a long letter but the mail will go
out soon and I want this to go for fear you think the time

long   I know we do when we do not hear from you   we are all well and if you were to drop in our hive you would find us very busy

Your Mother

From J. H. Williams

Homer Hamilton Co Iowa Oct 16 1859

Dear James

It seems along time since we had a Letter from you. We do not wish to tax you in writing long letters, but it gives us a great deal of pleasure to get short and frequent "notes" from you

We got through "haying" a week since,   had a long and tedious time of it for want of means   It would be play to put up the hay, but with the difficulties we labored under, we had all to work hard. The difficulties were increased by the early frost of 5th of Sep[tember] followed by others on the 20th &c   this compelled the secureing of hay a month earlier than was required last year. We have put up 125 to 130 tons Now that it is done, when I look at the small amount of money expended I can hardly see how it was done. I paid out only about 10$ in cash, and the work is all paid up   True I have used some other values, but so much of it has been managed by ourselves, that really but little was expended. It Costs me less than a dollar a Ton, including pay for our own Labor Which is much lower than it ever cost me before

The hay was put up on Racks last year, but they too are greatly cheapened while they are improved this year. You may Judge of the extent of the racks   There is 88 feet on the South of the barn, 120 on the West and 150, on the north (while the Barn is filled with same kind of racks, 120 feet in it)   Makeing the feed a complete protection to the cattle, while the[y] get it themselves, without attention on our part. I have not increased the number of cattle lately   every effort was turned to geting up hay. I have enough to make it safe to

"Lessons of humility and of humanity" · 53

rise to 150 head, If I get the means during the winter, which I hope I will, hence the effort to secure so much hay

Mother has just received a long letter from Grand pa. Much of it is about *Park[er's] shortcomings* and *spendings*, which have absorbed some $1300 of his fathers hard earnings, which he looked upon as the means of secureing his comfort in his declining days, should they be lenghtened out— Details are unnecessary It is sufficient to know that alcohol is the cause[1] In your letters to him, make no allusion to the melancholy subject. He seemed solicitious that even I should not know it. I thot all was not right, or he would not be liveing alone. we have urged him to come out here. His greatest objection is reluctance to travel on ac-[coun]t [of] the nature of his disease. We think however he will come before spring. I could meet him at the end of the RailRoad, and less than 2 days would land him there

In regard to coming home, we think your decision is best. I wrote under the influence of surprise, and mingled indignation, *Illy callculated* to dictate that discresion which is best under the circumstances of the case. The *insight you are getting, the amount of economy you can save* The *distance* and expense of the Trip and c[etera] make it well to consider well the matter

I feel thankful that you have sent the fifty dollars. It releives that pressure and I hope the sale of the Land will enable me to settle all soon. Cowen has got a decree to sell, and the Land will be offered in this month, so that I expect to Know the result soon— If I get money [it] will increase the stock now 66 head at least 100 more during the winter which is the time to buy here. All prudent purchases will treble themselves by the month of July or June. Which after one half the increased value is allowed for wintering is a hansome investment. This estimate is not based on the price that can be obtained by driveing east, but the price they will bring here in the summer. If you wish, I can profitably invest any money you can raise, and if it is wanted when you return in August, we can drive east old and young, and more than double the money after paying handsomely every expense

The frosts have dried up the wild pastures here a month earlier than usual, Showing the necessity more clearly for Tame [cultivated] grass for fall winter, and spring use. If that provision was made I do not dislike the lenght, nor the severity of the winters. The soil is so productive, and the climate so well suited to the thrift of cattle in the summer and fall months, that all that is wanted is the tame grass for fall, winter, and spring, to make it one of the best stock countries in the world, and when we look at the value of Land east of us, it is as near market, as cheap grazing Lands canbe obtained, and these rich lands worthless almost, in the present [economic] pressure, must soon command high prices, and be owned by a better class of citizens than we have now   Money is tighter than ever here. This stringency will increase till the country begins to swarm with sheep, and stock generally; when the money tide will set west—   The first step toward this is now being taken,   more than half the worthless population has left, or is leaveing, and will leave this winter. They are trading off their improvements & stock in many cases, *for old watches or anything* they can get and cary with them   Thus the pressure, which has been a great trial to the west, will prove a great blessing in the end   As personal trials, and Temptations purify the man, and brighten the character, so the difficulties here, are purging the country—   Stimulating effort in the right direction, and preparing the way for enterprise that will make it soon a great Country

Your affectionate father
J. H. Williams

From Rebecca Williams

Homer Hamilton Co Iowa Nov 12th 1859

Dear James

   I received your letter. We are going to school to Dr [J. J.] Miller.[2]   he is a good teacher but I do not like him as well as I did Mr Blair.   there are only thirteen s[ch]olars and they are all small.

The boys have been plowing out at the farm   Mr. Kort-
rights son was plowing and several others.   they have about
twenty acres plowed.

We have had the largest prairie fire I ever saw.   it was a
very windy eavning.   a fire came up from the south   it came
up to the place where Mr Prime lived and burnt a hay stack
that was there and the corn that was in the field and came on
up toward them. Mrs Smith got frightened and came down
here.   part of the fire when it came to Mr Dones fence took
up along the fence and when it got to the southeast corner it
went faster than a horse could run   it leaped . . . high and
got into Dr [Hampson] Corbins field. . . . Mrs Smith . . .
was running [to?] go and try to put [it out?]   in a few minutes she returned and said it had almost got into Dr Corbins
barn.[3]   Pa and John were out at a slough fixing a place to
water the cattle. Bella and Mrs Smith went after them   they
say where they were it did not look like a large fire at all.
they could only see smoke.   at that time there were a great
many men there. Pa took the mop.   they say that is the best
thing to put out fire.   he soon came back again   he said it
was no use.   the men had set a fire just at the road and it
could not get across the road so it had to go against the wind
and it could not go fast.   the men soon got the one nearest
the town put out.   the other past out by Mr Johnsons burning his fences and endangering his house and barn.   in a
little while we could see another one on the other side of the
timber   we could see the flames leaping up above the tree
tops.   it was the prairie fires we read of.

Rebecca Williams

From Bella Williams

Homer Hamilton Co Iowa Dec 17th 1859
Dear James:

I do not believe you could guess how many times I have sat
down for the purpose of writing to you, but I never could get

much farther than the date. I hope to be more successful this time.

It has been *trying* to snow all day, and I suppose a *Georgian* would think it had succeeded— But the snow is only a few inches deep on a level, and is drifting very much so that at least a third of the ground is bare, or nearly so. We have had delightful winter weather so far except one "cold snap" at the commencement, and there have been but three slight snows prior to the present; so that there has not been much sleighing or even sledding.

There is to be a "cotillion party at Union-hall, Webster City" on Christmas, and one at Mr Church's (this place) on New Year's day.

Flora writes to Rebecca that they are going to have a Christmas tree on Christmas eve and a party the Monday following— whether a *family* party or not she does not say.

I have been trying to have a flower garden ever since we came here, but have not been very successful. I had quite a bed of the Portulacca you used to admire so much, last summer and I saved quite a quantity of seed, about half of which I sent to cousin Frances. There are three colors,— scarlet, crimson, and yellow.

[?] sent me some Althea seed which I planted in a box . . . [but?] which ultimately turned out to be weed, and the other a seedling strawberry. The latter tho' very minute at first grew very rapidly and to my surprise put out no less than six runners during the summer, and spred over about a square foot of surface. I have often tried to get the seeds to grow but never succeeded, so I am going to see what this chance one will come to.

Mrs Smith gave me the seed of the strawberry-tomato so called because of its scent which has a strong resemblance to that of its namesake's that there difference cannot be distinguished. In appearance it is very much like the common ground cherry   the fruit is a bright yellow when ripe and of an excellent flavor; so at least she said.   for tho' I have seen them once or twice I never tasted one.

We also have the strawberry pea which came from the

same source: you have doubtless seen them growing in her garden. They grow to the hight of about four inches and their chief vertue is that they mature in about half the time as the common pea.

Dear James I hope you will not forget to come home as soon as you can, we all want to see you badly.

It is past eleven so I must bid you good night. We all send our love.

Your affectionate sister,
Bella

From Parker & J. H. Williams

Homer Hamilton County Iowa [1859]

Dear James

I received your letter a long time ago but I did not feel in a writeing humor   I there fore put off from day to day until I am almost a shamed to write at all. Pleas excuse me and I will try to do better next time.

I will tell you some thing about an elopement that ocured here not long ago   A young girl seventeen years old one day very misteariouslly disappeared. The circumtances were these. The girl was ill treated both by her father and step-mother who were in the habit of beating her with stove wood or whatever was handiest for every little thing. and would threaten her life if she told any one. But in spite of these efforts to keep it a secret some stories got out and her Aunt and others hearing this resolved to find out the Truth   they persuaded her to tell them. and being satisfied of the truth they made a plan for her escap. The first thing was to get the old lady and children off on a visit which they did   One of them went and got the girl ready. . . .

When her father found she was gone he was very angry and swor if he found her he would whip her until there was not a sound piece of skin on her boddy   He suspe[c]ted the

way she had gone and followed her but the people with whom
she was staying would not let him see her untill he promised
that he would not take her.   that is all that I can say.

Parker Williams[4]

The girl Parker aludes to is Clarinda Hartman. As I was
going to fill this blank I have been impolite enough to run
my eye over what he has written   If you can read it without
laughing you can beat me   It is Parker to the life, spelling
and all. He is so impetuous he scarcely stops to see what he
has written   He is learning fast however, As they all are, *But
John*, who strange to say, does not want to go to school and
we do not force him. He improved rappidly last session and
still likes to *read* but *dislikes school*. He reads well, is a good
Arithmatican [and] is quite expert in Geography, and has
improved in writing   It will do you good When you come
home, to see how quick he Bella and Parker will solve difficult problems in Arithmatic
   Dr. Miller is their teacher and will be for a year   [He is?]
capable but quite inefficient. . . .

[J. H. Williams]

From J. H. Williams

Homer Hamilton Co Iowa Jan 2nd 1860

Dear James
   I will add a word or two to Georgies and Rebeccas letters.[5]
This is a dry and beautiful winter, but too pinching– cold. It
revives my long cherished desire to go south. And were it not
for the *dangerous Magazine,– Slavery* which exists there, to
which any *Fanatic, Knave* or *Fool* may at any time apply the
"Torch" I would have carried out that desire long since;   As
it is I suppose I am doomed, the short remainder of my time
to these "inclement Skies".
   The stock does well so far but a great deal of provision,

and care is necessary for it, in such long severe winters,
True, by care in providing winter pasture they may be greatly
Shortened

Money is tighter than ever. There is none to be seen or
will it be again in this country, till wool growing, and Manufacturing a good part of what is wanted for home consumption are commenced.

No word from O[hio] since ordering to re advertise, and
sell at some price.

We intend doing what we can on the farm next year. This
will give you time to come home, and enable us satisfactorrily
to determine whether we will stay in this country or not.
Many things about it I like, but there are others I dislike as
much. I hope when you return we shall be able to take some
decided plan which will enable us all to act in concert, And
to be together. Union is strength but scattered disunion is
weakness,   Since you left I dare not leave home however ur-
gent the desire or the interest at stake lest amore direct interest should suffer. True it will not be long till I can have the
boys, or send them on buisiness But capacity is not all that
is wanted   judgement and Tact are needed and can be acquired only by experience. As an illustration, I ought to have
went to O[hio] this summer. I could have got the Land back
without the cost of a suit, and might have sold it so as to realize $500 to 1000$ more than I will after interest delay and
costs are considered, but I have [no] regrets on the subject.
The whole was seen but could not be avoided   it was impossible to go.

We will have all to buy for a year to come, and when the
scarcity of money is considered every thing is very high. This
however will be remedied the coming summer when we get
a crop— Still the great grieveance, or rather Obstacle to re-
maining in this place will still exist   The want of refined and
decent society   The thot of the children growing up, and
being confined in it, worries me,   They are doing well now
however   They have a good school and nothing to divert attention. We are trying to do our duty for the present, but the
questions refered to press with great weight upon us and

Must soon be decided. All that we can do is to act rationally in the circumstances in which we are placed— Then resignedly and contentedly submit to the unerring disposetion of Divine providence and Wisdom

Your affectionate father
J H Williams

From Rebecca Williams

Homer Hamilton Co Iowa
Jan 29 1860

Dear James

I expect in Georgia it is allmost like summer, here it has been quite warm for three weeks it is thawing and the water is runing every where. this is the first time there has been any mud since we have been going to school and it is two months and better it is all most like spring now almost warm enough to do without fire. there was so much snow that it makes it very mudy in places.

Pa talks of building out on the farm next summer but he does not know whether he can or not he says he will take the cattle out any how they are more trouble in town the people have such bad fences. he thought some of taking the store house out but he thinks now he will not that he will build a new one. We have two young calves George calls his one John Brown and I call my one Nina

I guess we will be left a lown next summer for there are so many people going to Pikes Peak they are all talking of going. A company started last spring from here to Pikes Peak but the most of them came back some of them went on to California and some stoped at the Peak Mr Hartmon Westly Hartmon and Squire Corban and Barton Corban and his wife went on to California but are not doing very well. Mr Mowry and his wife stoped at the Peak.

I will tell you our calves names the largest is Marmy Duk. Curly. Prince Albert. Queen Victoria. Princes Adalade.

Hatty. Cupid. Kates little calf.   old Brunts calf Parker calls
Moon, because he has such big eyes but he cannot see you
untill you are on him. Parker and I received papers from you
last friday

Bella studies Geography. Phylosophy. Grammer. Reading.
Writeing. and Spelling. Parker studies large Arithmetic.
Reading. Writeing. and Spelling   George studies small
Arithmetic. small Geography. Reading. Writeing. and Spell-
ing. I study Geography. small Arithmetic. Reading. Write-
ing. and Spelling.

Your affectionate sister.
Mary Rebecca

From Parker Williams

Homer Hamilton Co Iowa Jan th29 [1860]

Dear James

I received your letter agood while ago and was very glad to
hear from you. I thought I would write sooner this time but I
hurt my hand so I could not write for a week or to

We go to school to J. J. Miller. MD Five days in the week
and John and I acompined by Jackson and Leander Pemberton go to the timber on Saturday.   last Saturday we hawld
one load apice   sometimes we hawl two loads apiece   we
have harder times geting our wood than when you were here
in stead of going down to the timber and going to a tree top
and cuting our load we eather have to cut trees down or drag
them out of the ravens and that is slower work than when the
tops are down so you just have to trim them and load them
on the wagon and when we cut them down it is so heavy
to load

Mr Pemberton John and I went after flour last summer
to Henie[?]   John had Charley and Peet and we brought
twenty hundred and Mr Pemberton eighteen hundred with
his yoak of cattle   we had to traile at night   it was so hot the
cattle cowld not stand to be driven in the day time so we laid

by in the day time and travled at night and that way we got
off the road to Web[st]er City and went on the old road and
that was very slowgh   that night we traviled till the brak of
day   then we stoped to fight musceatoes the rest of the time
till morning and then when we got up in the [morning] we
didnot go over six to eigh[t] stepes till we were in a slough
but both yoak drawed our load owt when Mr Pemberton
came in   the oxen would not draw it out till we unloaded
part of it

About your dancing   I would like to see you dance   I
think it would not [be] very hard to make us think you were
our superiors in this art

Yours affectionately
Parker

From J. H. Williams

Homer Hamilton Co Iowa
Feb 13 1860

Dear James.

I take amoment to say that a letter just received from
Grandpa contains an offer from George Brown to give me
1000$ and 490 acres of land for my Ohio land. 375 acres lie
in Powsheik Co Iowa 40 to 45 miles west of Iowa City, the
bal[ance] to 80 miles northwest of this co[unty]. Now I do
not entertain a doubt but that in a few years, the land in
Powsheik, will be worth double the land in Ohio. The land
lies within 4 or 5 miles of the railroad which Mr Potwin [in]
Iowa City, says will be finished through that co[unty] by next
Oct. You may be ready to ask then, why not do it. The pressing want of money is what prevents. The 1000$ would do no
more than pay Browns own claim, taxes that have accumulated, Harris, and Cowens fees. Nothing left for debts here.
I owe 700 to W B Daniels and Co 300 to Woodbury, and
2 years taxes here, and cannot raise a dollar to meet any
thing. Were I to take this offer, I would have to sell off the

entire stock this summer. I then have some 15 hundred acres of land, and yet would be unable to get clothing, and comforts for the family— without means to act on. The stock if I can keep one year more, will be ready for market, which now it is not. When fed the productions of next year, in *grass*, *hay*, *pumpkins*, *Turnips*, and *corn*, with special refference to prepare for *market*. it will bring 4 times as much as it will this summer, and yet I may have to take the offer, as I fear I cannot otherwise sell it, which makes matters worse, as Brown's claim is added to the rest. Now in the event that I have to do this. If you will turn in and help me through, I could pay you by giving you half a section of land, I could not propose any other plan. True I hope to give each one a quar[ter] out of my present land which cannot fail to be valuable at no very distant day if I can hold on to it. But if you saw how we are pinching our selves, Mending up, and stretching old garments, so as to save to pay debts, you would wonder how we get along. I will write soon again, and tell you how we are doing in this respect.

affectionately
J. H. Williams

From J. H. Williams

Homer Hamilton Co Iowa Feb 19 1860

Dear James

In my last I gave you an intimation of our trials and difficulties, and promised in another letter to tell you something of what they consist of, and how we get over them.

Since you left we have not been able to get anything in the way of clothes, and shoes. The little stock of goods on hand, was soon disposed of, in payment of debts, and for help in puting up hay etc. in a living   You know how low watch work was— it has steadily declined since as the stringency of money has intensified   Last autum, I succeeded in laying in some 50 weight each, of coffee and sugar. The latter has

all gone long since. The former has held out and will hold
out, some two or three months longer, I need not say more,
as to what our trials are, as this will enable you to see them
all; And now you are ready to ask, how do you get along? It
is thus, Mother is all the time (when not cooking) remodling, and repairing, "*old garments*", which (aided by our wants,
and astonishment) she has the tact to make as good as new;
While John without "*Kit*", except a little peging– all which
he made out of something found on the watch bench and one
of my hammers has manufactured Mothers, Mine, and his
own shoes out of what? Out of old boots, and shoes thrown
away in the two or three previous years! Rebecca and George
too, have taken up the trade and you would wonder how well
they will fix up their own or perhaps their mothers, giving
out shoes! You may well be disposed to ask why we persist in
staying here? The . . . answer . . . is [that] property here
and in O[hio]– The Loss of all that I have Cr[edit] here,
has placed me in a heavy debt, compared with the means in
my power of raising money. Should the Land in O[hio] sell
even at a great sacrifice, this part of the difficulty will be
removed. An other difficulty, is, the danger to hea[l]th, or in
some way makeing things worse, by attempting to move a
large family. Again, I like this country better than ever, if a
start could be made in the line of industry suited to it, and
therefore hate to leave it, particularly as the land forms a
foundation for the movement. Again, I do not like the thot at
55, of starting my old buisiness, and geting a new stock, on
cre[dit], or By sacrificeing the land (The old stock being all
stolen) An other reason for not leaveing I want to take the
comming year to make a trial at farming, which has not yet
been done. We want to raise enough for home consumption,
and the development of our stock, which at the end of a nother
year, I must sell. if the Land in O[hio] is not sold; The effort this year will be to make the stock worth 3 to 4,000$
which if we succeed in farming, I think we *Will Accomplish.*
Again tho pinched we have good health, and are very comfortable, have a good school, and are in every way as well off
as our Neighbors if not better. we are not much troubled

about appearances particularly as we trust this embarrassed position will be of short duration. But all we suffer from it will be of great advantage to us, in many ways. It induces habits of industry, and Economy, teaches lessons of humility and of humanity toward the suffering, and indigents   It calls for the energies, and tallents, and a holy trust and Confidence in the Lord, which otherwise might not be exercised at all, or but feebly.

No letters since my last. Parker Rec[eive]d two papers Yesterday. We have no provisions laid in for the summer. The beef [is] of our own raising. Flour was purchased on ac-[coun]t of a prospective rise. . . .

[J. H. Williams]

Monday Morning [Feb. 20,
1860]

This is the most delightful winter I ever saw. Up to the most enthusiastic discriptions we have received of former Iowa winters. All the indications favor an early spring and a fine farming season. No shawls[?] except on a few days to be seen. Not much snow, no rain, and little wind,   Roads fine

Dont think we are gloomy from the ac[coun]t given of our embarrassments. We are far from it, and intend trustingly to meet them some-way

I believe I alluded to the great number from the west gen-erlly going to Pikes Peak. There is gold there, but notwith-standing, there cannot fail to be more spent than made the coming summer. A few with capital energy and an Iron con-stitution may make but the man will loose money, health, and character. The suden wealth of one in a hundred or thou-sand in a way so much like gambling cannot fail of direful re-sults on the masses who will congregate there compelled to work for or beg bread.

The suffering last year was great   it bids fair to be worse this year

[J. H. W.]

From Eleanor Williams

Homer Hamilton Co Feb 26. 1860

Dear James

We are glad to hear you are well and have so much healthful exircise and rational amusements   there is some danger of one of your temperment overdoing.   exerciseing too much at a time   you know we must be temperate in all things. How do you do at the dancing school?   do they make you feel that you are a plebeian?   or do you mix with them as an equal. I see by the [Augusta] *Dispatch* that some men have risen from obscurity to the highest honors in the state which looking through our no[r]thern glasses would seem impossible

We often talk of changing our location but though we talk we do not feel like exchanging our freedom fresh air and sunshine for city life   if we could have good society music and graceful intelectual amusements it would be delightful.   several families have come from Ohio and Illinois this fall and winter.   one has bougt the Remington place and two are living in town but they are very little in advance of those that have left

There are some very pleasant people in Webster City and if we were fixed out on the farm we might have company from there as well as Homer.

Mr Pemberton and Richard Fisher are going to Pikes Peak and Columbus talks of going though he is in the last stage of consumption and will have passed to the world of realities long before spring has spread her green mantle over the plains which they must wait for before they start[6]

Mr Butterworth has removed to Illinois to engage in some kind of mechanical business

We have been building castles (I hope not in the air) ever since you have been talking of comeing home, and Grand Pa has concented to come and see us in the spring.   in all of which we have a comfortable room for him and you and a nice observatory for your [spy] glass.   it seems to me we might be very happy with our frock [flock?] and herd grow-

ing round us and might have wealth and to spare   Pa looks
more robust than ever I saw him and seems to like takeing
care of the stock. I am well and more fleshy than usual for me
but think sometimes if I had some good Aunt Polly to relieve
me of the hardest work it would be to my advantage   the
children are all at school and it requires constant efort on my
part to keep them in order. Pa gave you the darkist side of
the picture last week   we are more confortable in some things
than when you left   the prospect for farming is better than
it has ever been since we came to Iowa   if we could get the
land sold and get out of debt we could do very well,   the
passers by stop to look at our cattle and ricks and remark
they never saw so nice a fix.   in summer our little place
looks more home like than any place in town   the green yard
in front and the little trees look quite pritty

Pa received your letter soon after he mailed his to you, and
Bella received hers day before yesterday   the papers you
have mentioned are all received and gave amusement to the
children

Your Mother

P.S. I must describe a scene that pased before my window
calling up pleasant memories   Mr [James] Porterfield lives
in Hancocks house and has been trying to make soap but
did not succeed   Mrs Smith has come to give advice or consolation or perhaps a history of her experience   the sun is
shining pleasant but a cold wind is blowing from the south
there she stands with an old hood tipt on her head an old
coat of Mr Smiths over her slim skirts reminding me of Davy
Coperfields Aunt Betsy and it seems as if we were in our
room at Uncles & listening while you read   Pa has gone to
sit up with Columbus to night   he cannot live many days

From J. H. Williams

Homer Hamilton Co Iowa March 11 1860

Dear James

Your letter 22nd ult. and that of the 23rd to Rebecca are recd. We all feel glad that Mr O[sborne] is so far disposed to do you justice as to raise your wages to 800$ Your Letters were begining to be painful to me as it was evident his supposed injustice to you, was fast begeting in your Mind a want of Charity toward him,   I am glad therefore, on his ac-[coun]t as well as on yours that he has— by this act set your relations on better footing,   It is often dangerous for us to be imposed on by others as we are appt to suffer more in our principles than in our purse by injustice   This teaches us how necessary it is that we should be careful not to view the character of others, through the colored glasses of our feelings, which is to judge of, and wiegh their character, favorabley or unfavorably, according to the favor, or disfavor, the[y] show us. This is the way the world judges; and it is indeed difficult to judge righteously of a man, if he does not favor us as much as we think we deserve. I make these remarks, because I know that tho't, and reflection in this direction, will be useful to you now, in *your forming manhood*. What can fill us with *more real heart felt unhappiness*, than to notice closely, and dwell on the weaknesses, and foibles, of our friends, acquaintences, and daily associates; this unhappiness will sour our tempers— cause contempt internally to be cherished, from which must flow, rude impo[li]tness to them, or a hypocritical politeness, which will be seen through in time, and in the end displease as Much. What then!   are we not to form a judgement of others? Certainly we are   every wise man must do so. But in proportion to his wisdom he must be careful that it be a righteouse and merciful one. To arrive at this, he knowes that appearances founded on isolated ac[coun]ts, on peculair hereditary tendencies, on a false education, or the influence of particular forms of society must be left out, or at least greatly modify the conclusion. This state of our being is a rudimental and formative one—   The body grows, Matures, and is thrown off– while *the spirit, the man*, is by action acquireing A quality which will be permanent. Now the *steps* of this process. are not all in the same direction whether the progress be upwards or downwards. The best make many missteps, while the worst seem to take some good ones. If it be thus with the two extremes of Mankind! How difficult is it, to judge justly of the mass who occupy the middle ground in Whom good and evil, are so to speak, more intimately blended. Now of all this, we must form an opinion—a judgement—and disconnect ourselves from those whoes association requires a sacrifice on our part, not of selfishness, but of principles;   You see then how difficult it is to form a just opinion of an other When our own selfhood as to be held in obeyance   How can those do this who never suspect any thing wrong in themselves, because they may be *free*, as *they think*, from the foibles, and faults, they see so manifestly in others? It is impossible! None can do it, but those who are suffering themselves to be taught in the school of wisdom– Who are looking to, and desireing to be constantly led, and enlightened by the Lord; that they may see more clearly the *secret motive-springs* of *their own action*. Those who do this will form generally correct judgments, always merciful ones. As they will hold no contempt for any one their politeness will be spontaneous– flowing forth freely. The soul of it will be *mainly Christian dignity* without the least aloy, of *sycophancy, insincerity*, or *hypocracy*. From *evil*, such a *mind shrinks*, while it leaves others to their own master, so far as there is no effort to make them do those things they see to be wrong   But a truce,   All this, and Much more, will be suggested, more clearly to your own mind, if as I humbly trust, you are looking to the *Lord for direction in the path of life*. That this may be your happy cause, let me earnestly entreat you, to read often and reflect much, upon the *divine word*. It is given in *infinite goodness* and *wisdom* to *lead* us to *heaven*

   We have just rec[eiv]ed a letter from Grandpa [Anderson] He will come by July, perhaps sooner if some expected jobs does not come in

Mr Cowen had an offer for the Land of 3100$ 2000$
down, but the man drew back when the day arrived   said
the man who was to have bought his own farm had failed
to meet his proposals. Brown offers me 496 acres in Iowa
326 of it in Powshiek Co[unty] and 1000$ for the land. It
would take the money to clear liabilities there, leaving 700$
[for] Iowa City and 300$ to Woodbury with two years Taxes,
and what I owe you of liabilities here! This greatly perplexes
me. My own feeling is to let that land go for anything I can
get, so as to pay off. There is no doubt however, that the 326
acres in Powshiek [County] will in a few years be worth more
than the land in Ohio. As Ma urges me to take Brown up I
have reluctantly concluded to lend two propositions to him
through Grandpa. First to take the 326 acres in Powshiek
and 1500$. If he will not [do] that to take his offer of the
whole 496 acres and the 1000$. In that case I must get time
of Woodbury and W. B. Daniels & Co. which I have no doubt
I can do. What will press worst is the Taxes   two years due
and a 3d one going on added to this   I cannot farm without
a team of horses–   The drudgery can be done with oxen,
but working corn and many other things on the farm cannot
be done with them to any advantage. Brown may not continue his offer as I did not take him up at once,   this will
matter little however as he must wait till the Land is sold for
his money so that I will be no worse off so far as money is
concerned.

When you write let me know what you think you can save
in the course of the year. If I do not get the time I speak of. I
must take the stock in the summer and sell it for what it will
bring tho it will be entirely too young and unfit for market.
We were glad to hear that you would send me fifty dollars in
this month. To meet the matters named I would want 200$
as fast as you can raise it. Taxes unpaid have 25 per c[en]t
added   But for two reasons, I would sell out and pay off and
go to a city Where I could do something   First I do not want
ever to buy jewelry again nor do I like at my age to return
closely to the bench again. 2nd I like the open air even more

than I used to and I like farming much better than when you left. The boys too are geting strong and like it. Stock farms cannot fail to be a good buisiness here. . . .

Your affectionate father
[J. H. Williams]

From J. H. Williams

Mon. Mar[ch] 12 [1860]

Weather continues fine   will commence sewing wheat day after to morrow   Stock does well yet to have nothing but hay   Columbus Pemberton Died first [of] this month. Illness long and part of the time looked distressing. I did not talk much with him. His father says he relied on the Doc[trines of the] N[ew]. C[hurch].   His conduct in some things looked like it. He gave a coppy of Nobles appeal to a young man where he was practicing medicine to whome [he] took a likeing.[7]

I gave a discourse at the house on the evening of the 2nd which seemed to lodge in the right place in some minds. There were a number over from Webster City

Judge [John D.] Maxwell wants to read   in consequence will supply him with a book of course[8]

Remember me kindly and give my respects to Mr O[sborne]

[J. H. Williams]

From Rebecca Williams

March 19th [1860]
Homer Hamilton Co Iowa

Dear James

We have had such fine weather a good many people a round here have sowed their wheat. Pa thinks if the weather holds he will sow his wheat. John and Parker are going to plow monday. We have planted our peas, and a few other things.

Not very long a go Sady Bell Okeson visited us. you remember her I expect. she was here and stayed two days with us. In the evenings we schottisched and played a very interesting play lately published in the [American] Agriculturist called the Bachelor's gift with many other things.[9]

The weather is so pleasant that numbers of people a round here are getting ready to go to Pikes Peak. it is only seven hundred miles from here. they get a yoke of oxen and a wagon then load the bed with flour and provisions. then they put a nother wagon bed on top of that extending out over the wheels. in this they have their bed and a little sheet iron stove to cook on with a pipe out the cover and the cover is high enough to stand up in.

Rebecca

From J. H. Williams

Homer Hamilton Co Iowa April 1 1860

Dear James

No Letters since my last. Do not expect to know result of proposition to Brown for some 15 days yet. The season continues dry and clear. No sloughs   Roads as good as in mid summer. Nights a little too cold or grass would have been good for some time. They are geting warmer and the grass will we think be a month earlier than last year but fine as the winter has been vegitation is kept in check   we feel that we [are fortunate that we?] are north. This has the advantage of keeping the fruit buds asleep,   the prospect for fruit were there trees would be all the better—   There has been but one rain [the] 22nd Feb since winter commenced. It is a fine time for ploughing and prepareing for planting and the boys are improveing it

Ma, Bella, Rebecca, Parker & Georgie have just returned

from [the] Methodist meeting. Mrs [Jeptha] Dewit still shouts for them when ocasion presents— Well she can afford to, Old [Barnabas] Dewit was caught by the hand in a wolf-trap.[10] His hand is about well. The trap was in the inside of [William F.] Wolseys corncrib set with full power, where it had a right to be[11] It would be easier to Tell you who are left than who are gone from country and village. This would not discourage us in the least, if we could get our feet under us in a buisiness point of view. On the contrary it is encourageing, as it gives room for better [people] to come in Walker is gone. Gifford, Butterworth, Meserva, Dr. Corban (but he will return in the fall) and manny others, (G. Gregory and Messmore run off Snell and Butterworth suffer, no one cries!) Some of them came in since you left. The Millers are all gone. A great number have gone and are going to "the Peak" this spring from the country

Fine as the weather is Stock require as much attention as in mid winter. (except as to water) The grass which gave promise some weeks ago is nipid back ever third or fourth night

Bella has recieved the [copy of Dickens'] *Haunted House* If the the season continues so favorable we will plant corn in this month which is early for this latitude. Have no house on the farm ought to have taken one of the houses out on the snow early in the winter there was a fine snow for such a job but I put it off other matters pressing then not fearing but there would be good opportunities again but I found we do not always have the amount of snow here which first experience led me to expect.

The girls and Georgie go to school Parker has stoped to help me. Parker ought not to be taken from it will start him again if well in the fall. Dr Miller does very well as a teacher but does not throw much life or energy into it. Our children however are studying hard enough. Others are doing little good under his management except Leander Pemberton

The village site still looks beautiful tho more than half the houses are deserted

I made a hot bed at the south end of the Barn,   have a
fine number of plants up. Rebecca & George made one and
planteded it yesterday
   Mon. Morn [April 2nd]   We often feel anxious about your
health since you have returned to the bench   Close confinement—active exercise, two extrems are dangerous. . . .
                              Your affectionate father
                              J. H. Williams

From Eleanor Williams

                              [Thursday] Homer April 19,
                                 1860
Dear James
   We have let two weeks pass without writing to you, every
day expecting to hear something from Ohio, but have not
yet: have heard from Grand Pa   he has been quite sick, and
is afraid he can not come to see us this summer, which we all
regret very much. I think it would benefit him if he could
   Many thanks to you from all for the beautiful shadow you
have send us.   if it does not deceive, you have not lost anything in appearance by going south. We are glad to hear your
lungs are stronger   Can you sing without getting hoarse.
   Bella has improved considerable in music though she has
not pratised much since she has been at school   She is very
hoarse from singing and feels discouraged,   she and Pa have
gone to Webster City to day   it is the first time for her   Rebecca and George are at school and John and Parker at the
[farm] place   so I am all alone.
   I am much obliged for the Haunted house   Dickens always gives a surprise   it is not what would be expected from
the title   [It] is quite interesting but not eaqual to his other
stories that I have read.   the caracters do not seem to live as
they do in some others
   Mary Hartman is married to the great joy of all the mar-

"Lessons of humility and of humanity" · 75

riageable gentlemen of her acquaintance, for she has been makeing great efforts to consumate what seemed to her the great object of life,   her husband is a lawyer [and] a good speaker   said to be quite talented   [he] has been teaching at Border Plains and she was a pupil [12]   he is a stranger   very little known about him

The Pemberton family are well but much broken down Columbus often expressed a wish to live to see you come home

[Friday] I did not get time to finish on Thursday but guess the news will not be stale to you

You say truly that you loose nothing by being debared [from] the society of the moneyed nobility   there is no real nobility but that of the mind and that all [it] can attain, who try [to] keep the thoughts and affections pure and are industrious, looking to the giver of all good for guidance and protection.   goodness is true greatness

We often regret that the children have so few advantages of society but are trying to lay a foundation by makeing them intelligent   Pa thinks sometimes that we will go to Webster City on account of the school   Mr Blair teaches there and is the best we have ever met and the society is much better than it is here   there is not a store in town now nor any goods we could not get anything if we have the money without going to Webster City or Boonesborough [13]

When you write let me know the Halls address   I wish you would ask Rachael [Jackson] to send me a dress pattern   it is so long since I have written [that] I do not like to. [14]

It would amuse you to hear the comments on your likeness particularly on the ornament on your lip. Bella exclaims aint he getting handsone? John says he would make a good Czar. Rebecca thinks it quite an improvement, Parker would have it shaved off, and Pa would rather see it on the chin, and I think it looks exceedingly well and George says, Oh, he has a mustash

Your Mother

From Bella Williams

Homer Iowa April 22 1860

Dear James

After such along silence I suppose I ought to apologize but
a letter I think will be as good an apology as I can make. I
suppose it is hardly necessary to say that I have received your
letter for you would conclude that I had any how. I have also
received several papers, which I believe Pa acknowledged
before

I went to Webster City with Pa last Wednesday;   it was
the first time I was ever there. We visited Mr Blairs school
and afterward called at his home, besides makeing severl
other calls at different places. Mrs Blair could not be called
hand-some, but she is very intelligent and pleasant, and in
my estimation a splendid performer on the piano forte. She
was formerly one of Mr Blair's puples, and taught school in
Wisconsin for a year or two, and to with in a short time of her
marriage, which took place some time last August.

Mr Blair used often to express a wish to see you; and I
know you could not help liking him, for he is so pleasant and
gentlemanly, and so unaffected.

Ma received your likeness—I don't know what else to
call it—last Monday;   we all think you have improved very
much in appearance since you left us, and we feel very proud
of you. Ma also received the book which you sent her, entitled "The haunted house". I like it very much, but not *so*
much as some other of the author's works.

The weather is pleasant, though the nights are rather cool
and we are sadly in want of rain, there having been but one
good rain since the first of February. But not with standing
these drawbacks the season is more foreward than any before,
at least since we came here, and many things in the garden
are growing nicely besides a great many things in the hot
bed, while last year we had nothing planted before the first
of May.

I have quite a variety of wild flowers in bloom in the garden; having obtained the roots on Prairie creek; whither I made no less than three trips last week,   I have also had the vase full of flowers every since the seventeenth inst.

I almost forgot to thank you for those watermelon and cotton seeds which Pa, of course, handed to me.

We all send our love.

Your affectionate sister
Bella

From *J. H. & Rebecca Williams*

April 30 1860

Dear James

Your letter of the 13th is received   that of the 11th containing check is not come yet

No sale or disposition of O[hio] land. I look for a letter every day makeing or declineing the trade for the Iowa land

We have cold dry weather   no rain since 22 feb. and that is all we have had since winter set in.   just the oposite of the wet seasons we have had

My struggle now is to pay the taxes which are going on the 3rd year   Land will be advertised in june if they are not paid. I will dispose of the stock[,] Land or anything I can to get out of debt   I cannot live this way   cannot get the children shoes nor any of the comforts they ought to have   I some times think I had better go some where to work if I cannot get away in any other way

We had a letter from Grand pa [Anderson]   he is troubled with *"gravel"* and will not without relief put over very long.[15] He could not stay alone in Town,   had gone out to the country to Parkers

Will write as soon as your note of the 11th is received.

Your affectionate father
J. H. Williams
Homer Hamilton Co Iowa

Dear James

To morrow is the first of May and we have vacation the whole month. it makes us think of May parties and May Queens. I am going to help them to plant corn the boys have been plowing for corn.

We have planted some garden. yesterday George and I planted our pop corn and some Melons some of the seeds you sent us.

Rolff is got to be very watchful the boys keep him at the farm to drive the cattle a way he is not so mischievesous as the young dog. Parker got a pup of Mr Church he has a red head like Rolff. We call him Don Estaban Oviedo.

You wanted to know how many families are in town that you know. Mr Pemberton, Mr Smith, Mr DeWitt, Mr Hartman, Mr Church, Mr [James] Hall.[16] that is all that remain here when you left. there is not one house occupied between here and Mr Smiths or Mr Pembertons. Mr [William] Sibert lives in Mr Daniels house and Mr. Porterfield in Dr. Corbin['s][17]

I send you our hight masured on paper and want you to send me yours.

Your affectionate sister
Rebecca

From J. H. Williams

Homer Hamilton Co Iowa [Tues.] May 6 1860

Dear James

Yours of the 13 and 17th ult. were received on the 27th & 29th. But no word from that of the 11th containing [the] draft! On the 30th I wrote to the cashier of Bank of Republic giving him notice that such a check was out in my favor in the hope that my signature might prevent payment and lead to detection should it be forged and the check be presented for payment

Tho I think there no doubt it is taken from the mail, I

think there need be no loss except of the $5   You ought to
see to it immediately

I have got through with the feed and seed I had to buy except about $9   I am now worst pressed for money to meet
Taxes   Two years have accumulated   Advertisements will
bemade next month adding to expense   This too when I am
unable to get shoes and some comfortable summer dresses for
Ma and the girls of the cheapest kind   I feel this loss therefore as a heavy one just now but I cannot under the circumstances think of you sending any more. I see your situation
is precarious   You may need all you can raise if you have to
find another location to say nothing of the risk of sending it
by mail.

You speak of some plan partly matured for the future   I
would like to know what it is. Much as I would like it here
had I a start I think seriously it may be best to find if possible
another place where I can make a living at the bench again,
and where the children will have better society. But we want
not only to know your plans but to see you at home before we
conclude any thing in the matter

No word yet from the Brown Trade under the last proposition. I look for a decisive answer daily.

No Rain Yet! But one since winter set in! Just the reverse
of the 2½ to 3 years previous. Has been very cold. Grass tho
a month earlier in starting than last spring is not in advance
of last spring at this time

Drop us short Notes often. The likeness is received. All
natural (and as good as a short visit) but that bl[ac]k circle
what shall I call it? Take it off and let the exceseve if any
grow on the lower part of your visage.

                              your affectionate father
                              J. H. Williams

                              Monday Morn[ing] 7 [May
                              1860]
a little rain last night   Laid the dust   seems very refreshing
after such a drouth

We have planted our Lots in town and are going to the

farm to day to plant corn   We are trying to do what we can
tho it is very discourageing   The distance to the shanty
is just 6 miles. Ive meashered it by the revolutions of the
Wagon-wheel. This, with the want of money, and no house
or fence on it, is very discourageing   The truth is we cannot
stand it, and will not try if I do not get something from that
O[hio] Land to give us aid   We will do what we can at puting in corn potatoes etc; but some turn cannot be made   We
will not pass an other winter here   that is settled

I will write to you as soon as I hear from Cowen or
Grandpa [Anderson] which I expect daily

[J. H. Williams]

From Eleanor Williams

Homer May 9– 1860
Dear James

We received yours of the eleventh containing draft yesterday, after haveing been sent to Homer Ga, and remailed from
there on the twenty sixth,   it will be some relief to us.   we
hope soon to be in a way to meet all our engagements

We have also received a letter from Cowen with a deed for
us to sign, and close that trade with Brown, wich we will do
as soon as the justice comes home. I have been very anxious
to make this trade   by it we get rid of one thousand debt
and more and better land   Pa wrote to Daniels and Co in
Iowa City to know the value of the land   they say the two
q[uarte]r's in Powshiek [County], can be sold in the course
of a year for 1,000 each in cash.   the [rail]road will be finished that far this summer, and a flourishing town two miles
from one q[uarte]r and four from the other will be the principal depot in the country

They are all out at the place except Bella and I and will be
all this week planting corn   there has been a fine rain and
everything looks promising for farmers   John received the
book and paper

Rebecca was delighted to get a letter from Rachel and will write soon

Pa was discouraged when he wrote last and thought he was troubling you for no use but is cheered up to try again, and if you can spare him some more with out disadvantage to yourself to meet his present pinch do so,   you know it will be safe.

I would write more but am afraid the mail will be gone

Your Mother

From Eleanor Williams

Homer 28, May, 1860

Dear James

Yours of May fifth eleventh and Rebecca's are received also a Magazine   I fear you tax yourself to send us books and papers. Pa and all but Bella and I are at the place   sometimes Beccie will walk out and drop corn all day   we are all so busy we have not time to get lonesome even in Homer.

We were somewhat amused at you[r] political demonstrations,   what ever is best for us and the country will be brought about by some means   Though it may not seem for the best to us short sighted mortals.   doubtless slavery has its use or it would not be permited and when that use is at an end it will be abolished. Bella is the strongest politition that we have   she wants a republican President elected to see if he will not do better and often exclaims "I do wish James was on the same side!   if there is any trouble we would be like the Virginians" then consoles herself with "but *they* did not lose their *love* for one another" you know"   Pa takes it very easy and there is no excitement here   there was a democratic meeting in town on Saturday   they appointed Mr [J. S.] Smith a delegate to Fort Des Moin, to appoint a delegate to Baltimore. Mr Smith keeps the Post Office.[18] Pa has got his taxes paid, and the deed for the Ohio land signed and sent on which I supose will decide the matter. we have the prospect of better times here. there is much more farming done the season is more favorable though rather dry

It gives us more heart felt pleasure to know you are industrious and faithful than to hear of your amassing wealth, for that is true riches, that will not take to its self wings and fly away, but will bring its reward, in time and in eternity, though it may not seem to be apriciated, therefore be patient and hold fast to all that is good. We are glad to hear you express the wish to make your home in the west the fear would sometimes intrude that you would become so much enomoured with the south and her institutions that you would not feel like returning to your western home, though humble it looks pretty now the trees are all grown and the garden is all cultivated it is decidedly the most home looking place in town

Bella has a letter from Maria Rion it tells of a flood eaqual to that of [18]52 in hight but much more destructive· having destroyed all the gardens between St Clairsville [Ohio] and Wheeling [Virginia] she also tells us that Mrs McNeely has been removed to the spiritual world You complain of want of charity in the church, it is lamentable that it is so much obscured by love of self, and love of the world, that the dense clouds seldom part so as to reveal it in its loveliness, but the Church is in its infancy and many of its receivers are merely intelectual and have yet to be vastated of many evils we must be careful that the want of it in the others does not crush the germ that is in our own hearts. We are not without amusements the children often go to the creek to gather flowers on one occasion they went with DeWit's children Bella was so engaged she did not see what was going on but hearing them call looked up the two Georges had climbed up into a tree and Rebecca and Rachel [DeWitt] had ran over the hill and were hiding behind one. the cause of all this was an anamal of Corban was coming up the ravene and of course they thought he was after them[19] they called to her to run but she stood and laughed at the ludicrous sene though a little frightened, and still laughs when she thinks of it   they came home tired enough and laden down with Lady Slippers and other wild flowers

Pa will write soon   I am affraid you will think this long coming but they have all been tired when at home   Since I commenced writing we have received two letters to Pa   one with [the] draft   I suppose you have received mine acknowledging the first one draft. We would like to have your [spy] glass but do not know how it would be safe to come   you must keep your old clothes to pack it   I would be glad of them to fix for the little boys

May 29–   This is a delightful morning   the girls and George commince school again to day

We had our strawberries on [the] Sabath and have peas almost ready to use   have had radishes

Your Mother

From Bella Williams

Homer June 3rd 1860

Dear James;

I received your most welcome and amusing letter a few days ago   I hope you will not think of comparing in any way a rough country girl, who can milk, churn, and perform many other homely offices, and, besides goes on all kinds of wild excursions; with one of "Miss Lizzie's" station. How absurd!

But then I do not envy her in the least, for I would rather be James Williams's sister than a *dozen* Miss Lizzie Osbornes.

I wish we were once more united on political questions, but I fear we never will be.

Poor Don got his leg broken week before last; he was out at the farm with the boys, and lay down under the wagon which they were loading with rails   when they started the wheel ran over his leg breaking it near the thigh– I mean breaking the thigh near the hip.

"Interests" is [the] nom[in]ative [case] to "suffer"—or, as it should be suffer, as I saw as soon as I read the sentence. You requested one of the children to give you the answer and as I am included in that class, and the only one of us that has studied grammar, I take it upon my self to answer.

The former Miss Mary Hartman—now Mrs. Hollyday—it is said already rues her bargain. She has not been to see us, or any of our neighbors for more than a year, which is only to be explained by the fact that all the young men had fled previous to that time.

Strawberries are just getting plentiful and plentiful they *are* O how I wish you could have some of our Strawberries and cream! then the pleasure of gathering them is equal to that of eating them.

Yesterday (Saturday) Rebbeca George and I went with Mr Pemberton's to Boon river in the wagon after goose berries, of which we gathered quite a quantity, but of course they were green. All kinds of wild fruits promise to be abundant, if the present drough[t] does not continue too long

Mr and Mrs Blair paid us a visit some time since. Mr B. had had several severe attack[s] of Ague which had reduced him very much. Their stay was very brief as they wished to return that day, and did not wish to be exposed to the night air. I like Mrs Blair very much though I think she is a *little* affected particularly in singing.

They were expecting her sister—a young lady of a bout my age—the next day but I have not heard whether she came or not.

The *Eclectic Magazine* and [*Frank*] *Leslies Illustrated* paper addressed to me, *Harper*[*'s Weekly*] to Becky, are received and we thank you very much for them. I like [Dickens'] Barnaby Ru[d]ge and Mordun very much.

We all send our love.
Your affectionate sister
Bella

From J. H. Williams

Homer Hamilton Co Iowa
June 10 1860

Dear James

Several weeks have passed, and a number of letters have been received, since I wrote to you. It is pleasant to hear so often from you, and as the times are so unpropitious here, the tho't that you are doing well more than compensates us for your absence. True, I know if we had even a very Small capital, we would all do better here. Well *patience, industry,* and *economy* will soon supply that. Little as is to be done, did we raise our living off the farm which we will do this year the shop will supply what would make us all comfortable, within the last 4 months, I have raised 75$ [I could?] not believe it, till I counted it up. [With] what you sent, has enabled me to lay in our *flour, feed, seed,* and *pay 105$, Taxes* by borrowing for a short time $35. Last year, we farmed the Lots only, and you know, *two, sometimes 3 flocks* of *chickens* for the *neighbors* have been raised on them. This year, we have a much better prospect in the Lots and there is but one flock of chicks to be fed. We have 40 acres [of] corn, at the farm, and a fair prospect for a crop. 4 acres wheat. We have planted over 50 bushels [of] potatoes covering 4 to 5 acres! You wonder what we will do with them if good, *feed them.* Had we had what this should yeild Last fall, and winter, our stock would have been worth 5 to 600$ more this spring than it is, tho it looks well now, as alw[a]ys on the grass. Added to this, we planted a great many pumpkins for fall and early winter feed and will sow a large amount of Turnips. Young stock, grow, and thrive, on roots &c [et cetera] better than on corn *alone*, and they are much cheaper, *cheap as corn can be raised here.*

Last August a change occured giveing [us?] the oposite of the previous two to [three?] years. Recently, we have moderate, seasonable, and growing rains. Grass is short, but crops look well, corn and potatoes fine. You may judge of the drought, by the fact, we could hall heavy loads to the farm last spring, with a single team, crossing readily the worst sloughs. At present the wheel makes no impression on them. We water our workstock at the Slough below the shanty from a hole cut 4 to 5 feet deep in the lowest part of it, in which the water does not rise nearer than two and a half feet of the surface notwithstanding recent rains! We have nothing but a shanty at the farm yet. It stands where you built the "*hide*" to shoot ducks. Now that there is grain in, it keeps work-stock on this side, and is convenient for water We have fenced up a pasture just west of the same pond, along [the] south line. This is the most promiseing season since we came to Iowa In regard to crops so far— The trees in the lot look well, but have met with so many "*Rubs*" [from the animals] they do not grow very fast. Some plumbs this year, tho there was a severe frost killing the cheries and the earliest bloom on the plumbs. The few plumbs [although?] green are very pleasant to look at. . . . Strawberries were plenty last year much more so this [year]. We have had many rare feasts enjoyed you can imagine where fruit is so scarce To day fine straw-berry-cake and delicious cream of which we have abun-dance we wish you here "*a little bit*," Mrs Smith is the "*Postmaster of this Little Villiage*", whoes hand-writeing you thot was, or favored Mr Pembertons

Hard as times are they will prove a blessing to this country in driveing a worthless improvedent class out of it breaking the mad-reckless-spirit of Speculation and giving a sound and needed lesson in industry and econemy and proveing the necesity of raising in the country all that is consumed e[x]-cept Groceries which the export of stock and wool will pay for and keep money plenty. But as it is we would get a long deviningly, but for the debt and this leads me to tell you what is doing to meet it and how much it realy is. I may put it in round numbers at $1100 independent of what I owe you It is not quite that interest and all but near so near it may be put at that figure. This money is going all but a small sum say 100$ to W. B. [Daniels] Co and Woodbury. They have treated me very Leniently but I will tire their patience. The stock may have to be sold to pay them. Tho I would like to keep it one, and part of it two years,　one year to develop (as most of it is young) and to consume the food which prospects are good for, will more than double its value. My hope is therefore to pay, by selling part of the land. I have sent deed to Brown but have not got deeds from him　trade not certain till I do. If it fails, I owe $1000 more. I think I can sell part of the land I get from him

I am to get $1000 and 3 quarters (This money goes for claims and expenses in O[hio]) and 6 acres of Land in Iowa or 496 acres 326 of this in Powshiek Co on the Railrod from Iowa City to Des moines　Road to be finished through that co[unty] in oct.　one within 2 miles of Depo, the other 4 to 5. I think this Land will soon be worth more than the Land in Ohio and upon full weighing of the matter I know I shall be well satisfied if Brown sticks to his offer and closes the matter by sending deeds. I wish I could keep that and sell land here but have no hope of that. . . . All caused by diappointments arrising out of that Ohio property and till it is out of my hands, I am not sure that the gloom is over, but I think it gone, and that the day will dawn soon in the payment of these debts, and then I [think] we will all breath free and feel that a great weight is removed

There is no one can work harder than we are all doing. We are pushing ourselves in every respect　we have laid out nothing except for provisions since you left.　of cource we are very bare. This can be borne no longer, and is what preses me, to move to some point, where I can do buisiness, . . . [If I went somewhere?] my-self and work a while in which time, I might be able to make some trade or turn, of the perishable property and look out a situation to move to. But as Mother has not been quite satisfied, with these views, nor am I clear about them. . . . I feel sure I can get time if I cannot sell but [I need?] 100$ in other hand and for money to get some immediate necessites for the family.　in all say $200—　now if you could raise me 60 to one hundred dollars, I think I can

Manage the rest. I regret to take any more of your money, I want to see you begin to save. . . .

[J. H. Williams]

From Eleanor Williams

Homer June 19, 1860

Dear James

Yours of the third and sixth inst are received   it is pleasant to hear of your improvement in music   it is not only pleasant to the ear but has an elevating tendency. I wish we could hear and see you,   as to good looks we can believe that   we all laughed at your attributing it to your mustache   I think those soft brown eyes have something to do with it   but beware of flattery.   it is the constant and daily performance of the common duties of life faithfully persisted in that forms at last a character that will stand the test of time.

We thank you for the trouble you take to help us and your present of forks will stimulate us to try not to retrograde which there is much danger of living as we do so much out of the world   Pa and the boys are at the place   indeed they are seldom at home except on [the] sabath   George has just come in for more provisions with the wagon and good old Peet and Charley and Rebecca is bespeaking a ride out with him.

We feel more encouraged and if we succeed in makeing the trade with Brown (we have not got the deed yet) I think we have passed the crisis. Mr Potter of the firm of Daniels and Co was here on saturday and is very anxious we should get it   says it is very valuable and advises Pa if he gets it to keep it a year or two,   thinks it will make money for him faster than he can make it in any other way,   he is certainly one of the most generous creditors   he told Pa not to sacrifice his stock but to keep them until next spring and herd up what provender he raises this summer, and if he wants more to use it he Mr Poter would furnish the money,   he always inquires for you very kindly   it is encourageing to be apreciated by such men.

Bella mailed you the [Webster City] Freeman   the storm there discribed was felt here but did no other damage than fill the garden with hay out of the stock yard

The last number of Frank Leslie['s *Illustrated*] is very interesting   [It] gives quite a good idea of the Japanese embasadors   this will certainly be a great epoch in their history, they will take home with them many new ideas, and judging from their characters will be able to profit by them.

You misunderstood my expression "You know it will be safe   I was merely giveing utterance to my own conclusion with out any refferance to how you would feel about it   never supposing you would stop to enquire whether it was safe or not,   we had another fine rain last night and every thing is growing so very fast,   in another year if nothing happens we will be able to say come home, and all can find profitable imployment. Bella is improoveing and if she had the advantage of a little good sciety would appear very well and would be a fine looking dignified girl   the boys need some rubing up but they are forming industrious habits and will improve when they have an opportunity

We have not had a letter from Grand Pa [Anderson] for some time.   the neighbors all inquire for you and have all been in to see your likeness   Mr. Smith will be going to Des Moines in a few days and we will send with him for the [spy]glass

Your Mother

I have been troubled with a numbness in my right hand and write with difficulty

---

From George Williams

Homer Hamalton Co Iowa June 24 1860

Dear James

When your lether came we were just going to sit down to supper all tierd and hungry Pa John and Parker had come frome the place Bella and Becce and I from Boon river we went in Pembertons wagon with here Bill and Charly Jackson drove the cattle. and the girls took old dresses and went in the river and tried to swes [swim] Bella could keep herself up in the water a little While.

I have not learnd to shoot yet so a gun would not be of any use to me they planted some sorgum but it did not all come up.

George Hite Williams

From J. H. Williams

Homer Hamilton Co Iowa July 8 1860

Dear James—

Yours of the 22nd ult is received. And notwithstanding a severe head-ache I must try to write you a few words— We are all anxious for you to come home— In case of not continueing in Augusta come home by all means. A new start if it must be made can be taken from here as well as from there. I would rather you would come home at any rate for reasons which I will state and let you judge of them— Mr Potwin of firm of Daniels & Co was here a short time since I had no trouble in arranging with him till next spring so as to have time to feed that portion of the stock that will then be fit for market During the conversation he hinted two or three times that if money was needed to buy stock in the fall I could get it. He did it by telling me how a man in Indian Town got money from them last fall bought cattle and paid some $600 to them, the[n] borrowed money and went home in the spring with two hundred dollars in his pocket. I took no advantage of such remarks except to say that if the turn out of feed this fall should eaqueal the present prospect the time would be all I want. With this arranged there is only one claim more of 300$ to Mr Woodbury on which I want to pay $50 for flour used (partly in the family and partly traded on my own ac[coun]t.)   The bal. $250 I can easily arrange. To this I must add another small sum to get "*inevitables*" for the winter and to pay a little bal. borrowed in settling taxes all which I hope to manage someway.– With proper care the stock will do more than pay the debts in the spring. I sent on deed to Brown for Land in O[hio] long since   have heard nothing since on the subject so that I do not know which I own the O[hio] or Iowa land.   Have written to Grand Pa to know the cause   I am not answered

Now tho I look on this Brown Trade as a good one, still I care little which way it turns.   Mr Potwin says one of the q[uarte]rs is worth $1500 and the other (in Powshiek Co) nearly as good. Which would make it a good trade without the qu[arte]r in Pockahontas [County], as it clears me of a $1000 liability in O[hio]. But if the trade is not made Cowen assured me he thinks there will be no trouble in getting the 28 to $3000 by giving a little time on part of the money which will pay all off and leave $1500 to $2000 to ac[coun]t on.   "*true*, except what would meet liabilities in O[hio] would have to be waited on a little.   but if the trade is not recinded I can be out of debt next spring with 1500 acres of Land in Iowa 326 of which is 1½ miles of M&M railroad (Miss & Mosouri) Which will be finished in that co[unty] in Oct   40 miles west of Iowa City   only an hour full time run. Now I leave it to you,   is it not better for you to come home and help develope these means than to work journey work where you can save but little after the closest confinement & appli-cation & economy and still more so if you must take a tramp to find the work. Times begin to right up east. The hard-ness of the money market here is in our favor in starting. My cr[edit] is good and with this property as a foundation I be-lieve there will be no difficulty in makeing a start if a judi-cious course is taken. What step should be taken I will not nor need not decide till the whole ground is viewed as it can be now in a short time when these trades are closed   but as I said it matters little what way the trade turns   it may vary our courses somewhat that is all. Now when you look over the whole ground— the time you have been away— The little you can save at best— The uncertainty nay the certain "*poverty*" of Tramping and the matters alluded to above is it not [wise to return home?]

[J. H. Williams]

From Eleanor Williams

July 26 [18]60

Dear James

Yours to Parker and George are received   we have all got a notion you are comeing home   Pa is so sure he says he will not write again until he hears from you and the children at school ask Bella what is the matter   she is in such good spirits   I do not feel so shure. We think it very warm but the thermometer has never risen over 93 at noon and the nights are invariable pleasant though we are suffering for rain   have not had a very good rain this summer   the grass is drying up.   there is not a well in town that is not nearly dry and Prairie creek is the same   the people are becomeing alarmed for their stock.   the corn looks well and there is considerable wheat and rye harvested. We are all greatly pleased with the glass   can see the farm from Pembertons and all that is going on there   while the boys were looking they saw a bird fly off the fense   John took it out with him thinking he could see Webster City from the shanty but he could not   it lies so low now   when they want the cattle they take it and look round until they find them and can then go right to thim   saves many steps

We had a Pic Nic on the fourth in Wolseys grove where we walked with you the first walk after we came here[20]   I have never been there since until the fourth   there were two

swings up and a table spread   all seemed to enjoy it. Bella
was dressed in white with green silk hosque and green on
her hat   Rebecca in white with wide sash and blue on her
hat   George with white waist and linnen colored hat and
pants.   they all looked very pretty   it was amuseing to see
the little country children contending for their hands in the
play,   John and Parker took a whole days hunt   left early in
the morning   took their dinner with them and did not return til dark   there were 150 at the grove   most of them
children: The [prairie] chickens are very plenty   John
brought in six last evening that they killed on the way home
excuse this I write in a hurry   it is past twelve and I am affraid it will not get in the mail

Goodbye
Your Mother

Numbers that went from here to P[ikes] P[eak]. are returning disapointed and sick   some have died

I think the neck tie you send John a great invention   why
did we not think of it

---

*The 1860 manuscript federal population census, which is dated
June 18, 1860, provides some clues to Homer's demography.
Williams's wealth is listed as $8,000 (real) and $2,000 (personal). He was over $4,000 more affluent than any other per-
son in Webster Township. It is not clear whether these figures
include the Ohio "deal" or not. Regardless, he was land poor.*

*The population of the township was 303, making it the sec-
ond largest township in the county. Boone Township, with
Webster City, was the largest, with a population of 463. The occupations listed indicate the movement of nonfarm people away
from Homer. There were 51 farmers, 14 laborers, 5 carpenters,
3 stage drivers, and one tailor, physician, miller, blacksmith,
wagonmaker, clerk, hotel keeper, teacher, and watchmaker.*

*Webster City's nonfarm occupations were as follows: 12 car-
penters, 8 lawyers, 6 teachers and merchants, 5 blacksmiths, 4*

physicians, joiners, brick masons, and cabinet makers, 3 hotel keepers, stage drivers, and shoemakers, 2 land agents, masons, traders, and ministers (one Baptist and one Methodist), and one foundryman, builder, engineer, tailor, editor, printer, tinner, butler, saloon keeper, druggist, machinist, stonecutter, brick-maker, miller, and brewer. The Webster City Hamilton Free-man, *on December 15, 1860, noted that the population of the town was 464, compared to 1,710 for the county.*[21]

THREE

"The storm that hovers on the horizon"

Homer has two or three mechanic shops, but no store. A school house is used for church purposes. There are six saw mills and two grist mills within five miles of the village.
—Webster City *Hamilton Freeman*, June 30, 1860

From Bella Williams

August 4th 1860

Dear James

Pa received letters of twentieth and twenty third ults. day before yesterday. We were greatly disappointed because they gave no assurance of your speedy return; but the knowledge that you were still enjoying good health somewhat reconciled us.

We have not heard from Grandpa for a long time and fear he is ill. Saturday evening's mail brought the deed for those two quarter sections in Powshiek county and a title bond for the one in Pocohontas [County]. Pa seems greatly relieved although it still leaves a debt of seventy six dollars *nearly*, in Ohio.

On the Fourth of July we had a picnic at Woolsy's grove. There were one hundred fifty persons present and all seemed to enjoy them selves very much.

John stood in the store door yesterday and saw four houses in Webstercity [with the spyglass]. They were probably in that part called "Massachusetts" as it is the most elevated portion.

A party of Indians consisting of three squaws, the chief

97

with eleven of his male followers passed through here on Wednesday enrout for Marshal county this state.

They were intelligent looking, and reasonably clean and neat. They had been up above Fort Dodg putting up hay and preparing to spend the winter there in trapping, etc.

They nearly all wore blankets over their heads   for all it was so warm and had enough "traps" piled on their hourses independent of them selves to smother both man and beast.

I have not time to write more and therefore must stop.   We all send our love ten times over.

Your affectionate sister
Bella

We get so many papers from you that I cannot acknowledge them singly

---

From J. H. Williams

Homer Hamilton Co Iowa Sep 2nd 1860

Dear James

Tho reconciled to wait a while longer before seeing you yet we feel anxious to know when you think you will be home! — As to crops we know now prety well the result   Wheat as a whole through out the state is good—   we sowed but little weeds had got so firm a hold of the soil I feard to do it and the little risked leads to no regrets—   corn, the crop is generally good and ours is good so far as we were able to manage the wild state of our ground. Potatoes very light. Pumpkins a failure and turnips will be nearly so. I name these things as you may see the state of feed dependence   It is not one third of what might have been reasonably expected had there been sufficient moisture. Added to this grass is very short— where 18 in[ches] to two feet last year it is in most places not 6 in. this [year] and very thin at that   under these circumstances to much is asked for puting up hay—   Have concluded to put up but little, and to take a lot of the stock east.

98

There are two reasons against this,   the stock is to young
and not fat enough, and the market is very much depressed;
The move will not pay off but will make the debt lighter and
stop interest

We have had the most singular year I ever remember to
have seen!   Drouth commenced . . . last fall . . . [and, though
rains?] have been frequent sometimes a few drops— again
laying the durt— next wetting surface ½ to an inch and occasionally to the deppth 2 to 3 inches.   Such plantings and
growing crops as happened to be favorably visited by one or
two of these partial showers (local) did well   others not geting them at the needed moment died overnight or came to
nothing.   But the season has been peculiar otherwise.   We
have had the hottest weather for several days I ever felt here
93 frequently 85 to 90 and yet with this heat there was frost
twice in the last month   killed nothing   The season has
been early in every respect   corn is made. When I look over
the casualties of the season The Drouth and Heat of Mo.
Kan. Texas 106 to 125 in shade & the consequent suffering
from failures of crops Iowa is far a head. She has by far the
largest crop ever raised. Springs still lower, now 5 feet to surface water in those deep sloughs!   dug our well 2½ feet
deeper. It bearly supplies the house yet vegitation Where it
has got hold is singularly rank from the frequent slight surface wetings

There are some things that press so hard upon me that if
you are not coming home soon I would be glad [if] you could
send me as large a draft as [possible?]. . . .   [I] will take
away some 35 to 40 head of cattle and keep about the same
number selected out of the young cows and all the heiffers so
that if we take proper care will soon have as many as we now
have

Our dependence will be corn & foder some potatoes and
Turnips for feed   have commenced cuting up corn. Ought
to start with stock but must secure the foder and have not
money to go yet!   I fear will be so late starting that the trip
will be a cold one and cost too much in feed—   now it would
not cost much. It is at times like this when some one is needed

here, or to go abroad   a boy will not do for either point except as an assistent. Such attention had we a little start would
in the cource of the year make and save more than it is possible for you to make by any amount of labor and economy in
your present position

We are very lonely but I beleive feel or at least suffer much
less from it than we did. The children are geting forward in
education particularly the girls   we begin to feel their presence not so much as children [but] as companions which releive us and inspires new hopes. . . .   [The?] boys are harder
to manage—   They [need?] more patience [and time than I
can?] command so that sometimes I get out of heart but when
I look around [and] compare them with others, and reflect on
the consequences of puting them to trade I try to be patient
and not try to shift my burdens onto other shoulders! Their
boyish days will pass—   They will learn to take hold of their
own affairs with the grasp of men—   But before this can be
done I have a trying time to pass through   The hardest part
is to be able to direct and govern myself   he who can do that
well can govern others

We all work very hard   Mother myself and the boys—
we are not able to hire any thing. All this begin to tell   our
prospects of being soon (I mean within a year) out of debt
never were better since this cloud came over us by the crisis
of [18]57 causing depreciation [of] prices and losses here
and in Ohio

But all things *Loss-Labor*. . . .   Tribulation of mind which
may be sumed up in the words *prosperity* or *adversity* will be
ruled by unerring wisdom for our[selves?] to [?] and commit
our selves to the [tasks ahead?]

Your af[fectionate father]
[J. H. Williams]

From J. H. Williams

Sept 9 1860
Homer Hamilton Co Iowa

Dear James—
    Yours of the 27th ult is at hand   We are all glad of your
determination to come home
    I think you should not think of walking so far as you pro-
pose after so long houseing & City-life   It is true, that where
you can save anything you ought to do so   I do not like the
idea of the expense of the stage as you will find *dimes* to be
Dollars here. I have concluded that I must dispose of a Lot of
the cattle unfit as they are for market, and depressed as the
market is at this juncture—   I will if well meet you on the
10th of Oct at Iowa City   will have a team to bring back
some things for the family   I have papers to record and want
to see the Land too—   Should any thing occur to prevent
this arrangement a Letter to you care of W. B. Danills & Co
will explain   Any thing from you to me near that time out
to get the Land direction. I would have to leave here by the
first. Should this arrangement fail on my part, you will find
the papers for record, and do not attempt to walk. But take
time   make yourself acquainted with the character of the
community— how soon the road will be made—   What can
be done in our buisiness— as well as the quality of the Land
    The numbers of the land are South west qu[arter] Sec-
[tion] 18 Township 81 North of Range 13 West in district of
land sold in Iowa-City containing 166 acres—   2nd quar[ter]
North East quarter Sec[tion] 3, Town[ship] 88 north of
range fourteen west
    hopeing to see you soon I will only add that I trust in *the
Divine* providence you will have a safe and pleasant journey

Your affectionate father
J. H. Williams

I believe the Crummy House is still a pleasant place to stop

Sep[tember] 10   All well. I am out of envelopes and rather
than go to get them I put this in an old letter

From J. H. Williams

Homer Hamilton Co
Sep 12 1860

Dear James

Since writing to you as I supposed for the last time a letter
from Grand Pa also yours of the 27th is received. Grand Pa
is geting better and will I doubt not come out with you if you
come that way. This will require more time as you will want
to stop a while at St. C[lairsville]. and at Wood Co. [Ohio][1]
When you learn what that time will be let me know when
you will get to *Iowa City* and I will go on and meet you. I
have to go there any how to get some things for the winter &
will make the time suit—   What you would have to pay in
the stage would help me very much in the opration

I am glad you are coming home any way   even if you
think it best to go back and it was to urge you to do so that I
used the remark "for all you could save &c,"   Some of the
reasons you cannot save much, I know, The expenses incident to living in Augusta, and I refered to these. You say you
can not save money, And I am well aware how easy it is to let
it slip through the fingers even of those who have the faculty
to do it so that at the end of the year, a large sum will be spent.
I refered to this too. And [I] do not see why the thot should
make you feel *bad*!   When I was young, I tried to save, and
did save something and I know how hard it is, to give the
close attention and time that I gave, and you have to give for
all you can save over. I think hard as the times are were you
here, and satisfied to stay, some way can be devised by which
at the end of the year, you would have more real value to show
and I wish to see the trial made   I think I can save money,
and yet when I look over the last 35 years of my life I see in-

stances enough, in which I should have laid restraint on in-
dulgence and expenditure,   without it, a man never can get
an independent start. But my greater drawbacks have arrisen
from letting others prey on me and here I will refer to a case.
Pemberton has got a considerable amount out of me.   flour,
money, & other values some of it lately.   some things were to
be paid in work, but I cannot get that.   At this time he is
makeing molases, & *cannot*, I think fail to have 100 to 150
gal. Yesterday evening, I asked for 2 or 3 gals   no he could
not spare any!   had I owed him but a small sum, he could
have got them if there had not been 5 gal left   The truth that
he deliberately intends to cheat me which for some time I had
suspicions of, flashed on my mind at once. I walked away
quietly feeling more pity for him than regret for my *loss*. I
have always been able to make money easy enough till now,
& even now, my stock cannot fail to make money, could I
keep it long enough to befit for market   I name the above as
illustrating the way my means have ever been filched and any
one who could in any way induce me to guard against it will
do me a *favor—*   I have written to fill the paper   There are
several things in your letter which time and reflection will
paint in other colers and set right   We would be glad to hear
when you start and the rout you take

Your affectionate father
J. H. Williams

From Bella Williams

October 1st 1860

Dear James
   Inclosed is a letter from cousin Rachel [Jackson] who, supposing that you were home directed it accordingly. It was
misscarried and forwarded, which, whith the time it has laid
here accounts for the long time that it has elapsed since its
date*

I have very little to say and less time to say it in and must therefore close my letter very abruptly. We received a letter from Grandpa [Anderson] sometime ago; he seemed in excellent spirits and looked forward to his visit (in case you came home) with exident [exigent] pleasure

We are all well and anxious for yet dreading your return to this cold, inhospitable region in such a season. In spite of the drought crops of all kinds could not well have been better. A considerable quantity of Imphee has been cultivated and the people are getting quite expert in its manufacture.[2] We planted some but it did not come up and the weeds took possesion. Pa had it plowed to prevent their going to seed; and it was again plowed, harrowed and sowed in turnips; since which the sugar cane has grown!

We all send our love,
Your affectionate sister;
Bella

*Seeing where it was from we took the liberty of reading it; which please excuse

---

From Rebecca & Bella Williams

Homer Hamilton Co Iowa
Nov 1 1860

Dear James,

We have had very pleasant weather.   Pa has been diging potatoes but he did not get them finished.

All go to school except John and Parker; our school will be out in two months.

You told us how you spent the day. I will tell you how we spend ours in the summer. George and I would get up about six oclock, eat our breakfast, then help to milk, get ready and go to school. Then about four in the evening run home, and if you were passing about that time you would see a little boy and a girl with spy glass in hand mounting to the house top and look over the prairie's to see which way the cow's, were, then booth come down and away after them and return about sundown with a drove of cattle.

There has been some large prairie fires this fall   they have been mostly out north. One day Pa and the boys went out to the farm to burn round it but they found it was burnt round and the hay they had cut—about four runs—and five shocks of corn, were burnt

I will tell you the names of our calves. Polly Hopkins. John Brown. Copic. Cook. Frisky. Violet. Jenny Lind. Lilly Dale. Western Bell. Quince. Blanche. and Betty.

Becky.

Dear James

As Becky has not filled the page I thought I would add a few lines.

Pa rec[eived] your letter of 17th ult last Monday. I forbear remark. At the same time I received a letter from Nelly who complains of not having been able to get answers from you since last March

She, Fanny, Rudolph, Emma, Adelia and Demming witnessed the "inauguration of the Perry statue" at Cleveland, and spent a week at East Rockport, [Ohio.][3]

Uncle George [Williams] is going to move to Toledo soon and engage in the broom manufacture.

At the time she wrote—Oct. 21st—Uncle was about starting for Schentady N.Y.; she did not say what for.

The weather was pleasant *until* last Friday. when it rained and continued showery until Saturday evening. Sunday and Monday were pleasant with the exception of high wind; and it has been windy, cold, and showery ever since.   Today— Thursday—a few snow flakes fell but soon were lost in the rain.

The potatoes are not more than half gathered and, I fear they will frieze in the ground.

Yours with great obligation
Bella

Nov 2nd It is snowing hard this morning but the ground is
not frozen

From Bella Williams

Answered Nov 25 [James's
handwriting]
Nov 12th 1860

Dear James

Ma's and pa's letters of 28th and 29th ults. were received
yesterday—I meant to say day before yesterday—and seemed
to scatter the clouds that abscure our horizon, for the time.

There is nothing new, except that I discovered the other
day for the first, that I am to be the school teacher this winter
and that our neighbors are highly delighted; and, more than
all I have already obtained a certificate of my ability from Mr
Blair! I suppose it is scarcely necessary to state the fact that
the late bearer is Mrs Smith and that she had it from Mrs
Porterfield and Mrs Porterfield had it from "dear knows"
who. The people here are anxious to have a school this winter,
and as there are no funds in the treasury they will be obliged
to get some one that can afford to wait a year for their pay.
If they *should* wish me to take it I will.

I said there was *nothing* new but I forgot. [Gabriel] Miller
and [Hiram] Chancy got home from Pike's Peak yesterday.[4]
They are as poor as could be wished. They with some others
are charged by Maricle wih having committed a penitentiary
offence against him.

As his saw-mill had yielded him nothing he could not pay
them then and wanted them to wait, but they would not; he
then sold his team and paid them off. They then turned on
him and threatened to lynch him if he did not give up his
papers; which as he was alone he was obliged to do. Mr M.
has not yet returned. This *too* came through Mrs S[mith]
and I have given it to you for what ever, in your estimation it
is worth.

It was snowing I believe when I last wrote to you! Well! it continued to snow for three days but until the last day it thawed almost as soon as it fell; on the last of the three however the ground was frozen and it lay at the depth of several inches for a day or two. The weather is now beautiful, moderately cool, but the ground is very muddy. The frost did not go deep enough to injure potatoes and turnips. Pa, the boys and three hired hands were out diging them on Friday and Saturday and have gone out again to day. They will soon be done with them.

We have received several Frank Leslie's [*Illustrated*] and Neonse(?) journals and a Harpers weekly within a short time. I think it is unnecessary to put so much postage on them as you do. I received two Frank Leslie's from Nellie the other day and each had only one cent on, which, Mrs Smith (our Post Master or rather Post Mistress) says, is all that is necessary for any paper no matter what the size. It *may* be different in Georgia though.

I supose you will be installed in your new home [in Mobile, Ala.] by the time this reaches you. I hope you may be happy in it.[5]

I believe that is all.   Your affectionate sister,
                                          Bella

I received a letter day before yesterday from Emma Rudolph; they are all well and so are we.
                              B.

From Rebecca Williams

                    Homer Hamilton Co   Iowa Nov 16 [1860]
Dear James,

I suppose you are in your new home [in Mobile] by this time. We are anxious to know how you like it and the people you find there.

Last Wednesday Pa Bella and I went to Webster City with

Pete and Charly. We wanted to go the surveyed road that
goes past the farm.   so we went our road till within a mile of
the farm when we struck off into the new road. It had never
been traveled and the oxen had no notion of going with out a
track to follow.   so it was not very easy to keep them right.
but that was not the only trouble   the stakes were pretty far
a part and it was difficult sometimes to distinguish them at a
distance from the big weeds. We arrived there after three
hours of riding in the wind   Went round the town a little
[and] made our purchases.   and a bout four o'clock started
for home. As it was late we did not attempt to follow the new
road and therefore went home much faster then we came but
we had two or three miles farther to go. We came the lower
road and got home about eight o clock.

The weather has been very pleasant since the storm untill
to day it blowes very hard and is cloudy.

Your affectionate sister.

Becky

From Bella Williams

Homer Hamilton Co Iowa Nov 25th 1860

Dear James;

You are doubly dear now that we have lost you, but when I
look at the sweet face of the daguerreotype you sent I do not
wonder that you love Miss ["Lizzie"] Rennison. I feel that
she is as dear to me as a sister already.

Since your letter came announcing your intended marriage, we have not been able to think of any thing else.   and
Becky wakened me the other night by talking of her in her
sleep. To cap the climax, I have serious thoughts of going
through a bleaching and beautifying process, and then when
I have acquired the requisite brilliancy and beauty of com-
plexion I'll send you my daguerreotype, so please live in hope.
And then too I will have to improve my disposition   Odear!
Odear! what a task I have undertaken!

Pa and the boys are going to Marshalltown as [soon as] we

can get them ready—probably Monday week—to dispose of a portion of the stock.[6] Mr Woodberry is going to take them for the debt. Pa will take the deeds of the land in Powshiek Co. and have them recorded, and may possibly go on to Iowa City

Pa has not written to you for a long time. but his mind is so ocupied trying to devise means to get out of debt and get fixed comfortably that you must try to excuse him. Ma is very busy too but will write soon. We got our potatoes and turnips all saved. The weather has been very cold for the past week, but we cannot tell the exact temperature for John carelessly hung the thermometer on the north of the house— the wind blew it down and broke it. we are very sorry more particularly so because it was a present from *you*.

Our school came to an end last Friday. You say the "days of the Union are numbered." Granted but not "*few* and numbered," I hope.[7]

Pa received your letter of 10th inst last Friday. he also received two or three a short time be for— and Ma, one As to papers, Oh! I cannot enumerate *them*, but you may take it for granted that we receive them, read them and thank *you* with all our hearts; but Pa sometimes objects a little saying "you are too prodigal with your money, for you know the proverb says "take care of the pennies and the dollars will take care of them selves".

I wish you much joy.

Bella

P.S. I admire the pattern of the collar you sent John very much and thank you for him; also for the [Dickens] book entitled "A tale of two Citys." I can hardly say that I like it, though it is well written.

I wonder if you receive all our letters! I have written every week for at laest a month and a half and Pa and Rebecca have each written several times since we knew you were not coming home.

Bella

From Eleanor Williams

Homer De[cember] 2 1860

Dear James

We received yours to Pa, and George of [Nov.] fifteenth, and sixteenth, from Mobile, and feel relieved to hear you are safe at your new home, hoping it will prove a pleasant one. doubtless it will have its trials, but if they are met and overcome if possible, if not borne, they will elevate and purify, for trials and temptations are permitted only for our good.

The announcement of your intended marriage was quite a surprise to us   we had not thought of you entering into that state so young, that you would wait until you were better established in business   but a good wife is one of the greatest blessings a man can posess and if you are economical it will not retard your worldly advancement while it is a beacon pointing upward and onward.   at first we felt like step children and jelous that any one should come between us and you but we have put away that selfish feeling and long to welcome her to our little circle   certainly that sweet young face of hers is like a letter of recommendation   as to connections it is pleasant to have good and influential friends but it is purity and goodness that are true riches that will not take wings themselves and fly away   a good character is above all things else

When you get your wife perhaps you will have fulfilled your mission to the south and will come home and build a house on some of the land and live among us.   we hope to see you next summer at any rate

Mr Osborne['s] parting gift is gratifying not on account of its value but it shows he was satisfied with your course

Pa and Parker have gone to Marshal[ltown] with eleven head of cattle, to pay our indebtedness there,   they started on Thursday and expected to be gone seven or eight days. our town is as dull as ever   we seldom go out but we are all kept so busy that time passes fast enough   we will have no school this winter but intend to have the children studdy at home   I thought if Bella and John had an Algebra with a key they could get through with out a teacher   Bella advances very fast in all she undertakes   Dr Miller says he never saw any one master grammer as she has done but she has been kept so busy with studdy and helping she has not had time to attend to her mind

That the Lord will guide and direct you in all that you do is the prays of your

Mother

From J. H. Williams

Homer Hamilton Co Iowa Dec 10 1860

Dear James

Yours of the 22nd ult. and several previous letters are received, also one to Bella dated the 25th. The hope of seeing you in the begining of Nov. your change of location and my absence of a week in Marshall Co has caused me to leave writing to the children

I regret to hear you say in regard to the disolution of the union, that the sooner it occurs the better.   The letter is not before me but this is the amount of what you say.   When you are older, are cooler, and have duly weighed what it cost to establish American independence; and when you have fully passed in review all the advantages, and blessings, which have resulted from the union of these states; I think you will not lightly give vent to such utterances. I know They are becoming common in certain circles north as well as south; and what strikes me as passing strange in all this, *is*, that the parties in the north and the south who are uniting to produce this result, are acting from different motives—   The one for the greater security of the peculiar "*Institution*," The other to remove the protection which the federal Constitution and laws throw arround it   They think these barriers broken down, the Canada line would at once move south to the Mississippi and Ohio Rivers, when it would not take long to place it on the southern line of Tenessee, Kentucky, Virginia

and Maryland which would includes Missouri of course
what blood and carnage such views contemplate and yet
those who hold them affect to believe it would take place
peacefully   How can *extremes so oposite laboring* to *disolve
this glorious union, omen* a *peaceful* or *happy settlement* of
such *momentous* a *question*!!!   I never was an abolitionist
never had any sympathy with them   Always thought them
insane and visionary. I have at different times viewed the abstract subject of slavery in different lights, as I have most important subjects which have continued long to be the object
of thought;   And I may say here, that I have never decided
any thing in regard to it, but what the constitution decides,
that it belongs to the state in which it exists to regulate it in
its own way. But a truce to this,   will The union be disolved?
That is the question!   I hope and believe it will not—   On
the contrary the present storm sever[e] as it is will I trust be
most healthful! It will disperse the miasmas that have settled
in the political atmospher—   The smoke will soon be above
the mountain tops when all the parts of this great nation will
see distinctly the interest they have in the union, and the
benefits and blessings it secures and bestows on each—   And
better still, I trust they will beable to discover the true paternal feelings which have for a time been obscured by the *dust*
raised by interested and frothy poloticians North and South
which have without authority spoken in the name of their
different sections. The peoples estimate of the union, the
grievences they suffer, and the mode and measure of redress
they desire, has yet to be stated. Noisy poloticians must stand
aside till they are heard in their primary meetings and in
their conventions by their chosen representatives. It would be
the greatest political folly to act without this expression! It
would be to put reins into the hands of those who unable to
govern themselves must by their mad councils involve the nation in all the horrors of civil war $=$ *servile insurrection* $=$
plunder and *Liberteneism*!!! But will not these same poloticians influen[ce] the peoples expression in their primary
meetings and conventions? To some extent they will, but
they will be unable to precipitate them into rash action Greiv-

enances will have a clear presentation. The duties of delin-
quent States will be pointed out and will be seen and acknowledged by all no Matter who is president. When this is done in
a fraternal and dignified Spirit restassured The good men in
all parties will in their might put an end to the evil of whatever
character it be, whether it pertain to the legislation of the
state, or to conniveing at the operations of the underground
railroad[8] When the feelings of the great heart of the nation
thus get leave to speak out, I do not fear the result— *All will
be well* The constitution will be better understood and its
Obligations will be more faithfully discharged While its
benefits will be more generally appreciated! I believe all this
and much more than I can crowd into the comfines of a letter
will be brought about by the present fiery trial of the working of our System of Government! I believe the country will
come out of this ordeal more affectately united = More disposed to let each others interests and institutions alone, and
more ardently attached to the Constitution as it is— the
combined wisdom of the fathers of our country— than would
have been possible had these troubles and trials never been
experienced. The present storm I hope will end in thus ce-
menting and uniting more firmly in paternal relations the different parts of this great nation instead of scatering it into
rival and contending fragmnts; and I believe too, he is the
greatest patriot and friend of man, who throws oil on the
troubled watters, and labors hardest to bring this about! How
well Hon. A. H. Stevens has done this in his able speech before the Legislature of Ga;[9] But you say he is a polotician!
Not in the sense in whch I use the term— He is a statesman
who understands because he studies the wants and feelings of
his countrymen and when he speaks He embodies and sets
forth those feelings and wants! You will see how truly this is
so, if you read the proceedings of some large meetings lately
held in *Ga.* The result is, that instead of rash action a convention is to be called, not to devide the union first, but to
array in clear light, the greivences that if not redressed, the
union will be disolved. Let this be done as Mr. S. says in a
becoming spirit as I have no doubt it will, and all is safe, or

real grievences will be redressed; and imaginary ones will vanish in the effort to establish them. This is the way to settle rationally these matters. This course will anilhalate the power of afew fanatics at the no[r]th who ardently but secretly desire the disolution of the union that they vainly think might have a better chance to distinguish themselves as heroes in liberating the slaves of the south while they could enrich themselves by plundering their masters. Now I donot think there is such a man if there is one in every one thousand of the inhabitants of the North. But let sectional difficulties commence and what power would such have. How easy to raise bands every where among the idle vagabond crew of every land, ready for any thing? You will not be surpised then when I say I have little faith in the political Segacity of those who look for a peaceful secesion and a sucessful career thereafter. They show little polotical foresight and little knowledge of the history of the past! When and where has a great nation been Sundred and such results followed? As well expect family peace and prosperity amid family broils and contentions? Do not such divisions engender endless suits in which all is lost— both as to character and property? So it has ever been with the *severed-heated-contending elements* of once great nations! They never settle satisfactorily their boundries and their thousand and one international and individual rights! There is always some pretext to justify the operations of freebooters, at least in their own estimation and that of their infatuated followers!

But dark as the storm is that hovrs on the Horizon I trust in the Divine Providence   it will pass away   the calm that will follow will be all the plasanter, and better appreciated

There is another important subject that I wish to notice to which you have called attention but I have spent so much more time than I intended that I have concluded to reserve it for an other letter

Your affectionate father
J. H. Williams

From Rebecca Williams

Homer Hamilton Co Iowa Dec 23 1860

Dear James,

I received your letter and I think I felt a little proud of it for it had been so long since I had received one from you. I had not written for a long while.

It is very cold but there has not been any hard storm since you left. The sleighing is very good.

Pa got all his potatoes in with a great deal of labor but I am afraid they will frieze in the cellar.

George and I have a yoke of calves that we call Jake and copice. One morning we yoked them up and went to the steam mill for a load of wood. I got on the sledge and George drove them. We gathered little bords and sticks   got a load and started for home.   but this time we both got on. They trotted a little while but soon got to walking.   George laughted so he could hardly sit on the sledge. When we got up to the stockyard fence Jake wanted to go in and George had to get off.

John has a yoke of two year olds and Parker a yoke of one year olds. One after noon they hitched them up to go to prairie creek   George and John went to gether and Parker and I. Parker walked all the way down but said he would ride coming back. We did not get any wood but John said he would not go back till he did.   he went on, but we turned back. when we got out on the prairie Parker got on   I got fixed as well as I could but it was only a little hand sledge and there was not mutch room   they started upon the trot and then into a lope and I roled off b[e]hind, and Parker came pretty near doing the same, but he grabed the hind bench of the sledge and was draged a long in the snow. When I got up I looked to see where he was and I saw them near the Des moins road going as hard as they could. Pretty soon I saw he had them. I tried to catch up but they broke a way from him and started home   they ran against a post and stopped.

I expect you will laugh at me but if you and Lizzie come
out here you may have a ride with me.

Becky

From George & Bella Williams

Homer Hamilton Co Iowa Dec 26th 1860

Dear James

I though[t] I would write to you. The snow is just about a
foot deep and some place it is deeper. The sledges are going
pretty near all the time.

John and I went down to Prairie creek to get a load of
wood with a yoak of two old stears. We got down in the bot-
tom and did not see any good wood. there was a little dead
buroak up on the hill and John said that he would go and get
it; it was burnt down and we loaded it on the sledge and
started towards home. We went about ten rods when the off
runner hit a little nole [knoll], and threw the wood to the
near side and the runner b[r]oke down, we managed to fix
it so we could ride home on it. When we got on to the road
we both got on the sledge and John told them to go and they
started on the run when we came to Corbins lane, they
started on to the bridge but be-fore we were quite a-cross it,
they turned off and jumped a ditch four feet wide and ran into a fence corner and stopped, and John got off and caught
them, and John got on a gain and they went right along the
road

George Hite Williams

Dec 27th

Dear James

We had a merry Christmas, and I hope you had, and Lizzie
too. We spent it at Mrs. Smith's (they live where they used
to, but do not keep tavern) who relieved of all apprehension
of being burdensome, by setting us all to work to help her—
of course we had been invited but I suppose you have had a

feeling some times that you had been invited mearly to save appearances? I know I have had, but *not last Christmas*. Well we had an excellent dinner at three o'clock, of which a seventeen pound turkey was the most conspicuous, a "taffy (I dont know whether that is spelling right or not) pulling" in the evening, and then we played "Bachelor" and "Quaker" till ten o'clock, when we had a lunch, and then waded home through the snow, to a cold house and tumbled into equaly cold beds, slept till five, and then tumbled out again to go through the daily rotine.

You must excuse the mistakes in Georgie's letter, for if I should tell him he might improve it by writing it over   it would almost break his heart.

On the 23rd we had the quietest and heaviest fall of snow I ever witnessed even in this State of wonders and it continued calm until yesterday evening when the wind—which was coming from the south east—rose and the snow began to "kelter" and has continued to do so since.   but though it is drifting a good deal it does not fill the air so as to blind one.

[Bella]

From Bella Williams

Homer Iowa Jan. 6th 1861

Dear Lizzie

May I presume to call you "Lizzie" dear sister? or do you think "Mrs. Williams" would be more appropriate? I must confess *I* do not, and will therefore call you Lizzie, at least until requested not to.

When James sent your daguerreotype accompanied by a letter acquainting us with his intended marriage.—which we learned by day-before yesterday's mail was consumated on 14th ult—and speak in such high terms of you.

I felt so enthusiastic, that I determined to become acquainted with you thro' the medium of the post, forthwith; but when I saw my poor scrawl on paper, was it any wonder

I turned away saddened and disgusted? I think now; but I thought of you both, constantly, and morning and evening breathed a silent but heart felt prayer for your happiness.

I gave James an account of our Christmas from which you will no doubt draw the inference that our amusements are very primitive and tame—my description was certainly the latter—and probably they are; but we never the less enjoyed our selves hugely on the occasion referred to—or at least *I* did.

New Year's was a most beautiful day and we had a sleigh ride which we enjoyed as much as our sense of the beautiful and delicious would admit of.

There was a public ball in the evening. but tho' we believe dancing to be harmless and pleasant *in its self*, yet we have grave objections to the persons who invariably attend such gatherings here; and therefore we did not go.

Our houses are surrounded by immence banks of snow, but on the open prairie it is pretty equally distributed. Soon after the snow fell we had a very heavy sleet which secured the snow from blowing and made the surface of the drifts as smoth and firm as could be desired, affording a fine opportunity for sliding, which Rebecca and George have improved to its full extent.

It is cloudy today, and is thawing some. Ma and Pa, indeed all of us send our love.

Your proud and happy sister
in law,
Bella

P.S. I wish to add a few lines for James.

Dear Brother, I wish you joy! O how I wish I could see you and Lizzie and talk to you! this way of putting ones ideas on paper seems so senseless, and I cannot express half what I want to, so I will leave you to imagine the rest.

I believe I told you that Mary Hartman married Mr. Holoday, which was a mistake. her husbands name being Ammond. The misunderstanding arose from the fact of their both being lawyers; both teach in the same neighborhood, each marrying one of their puples, and being married at a bout the same time. Mr. Ammond is very gentlemenly and appears to be well educated. I have seen him several times and the oftener I see him the more I wonder what could have induced him to marry her. They were only acquainted three month[s]. part of which time he was sick and she took care of him.

I send you a "poem" written by him, which, by the way don't speak much for his poetic powers; the theme is the post office at Webster City about which there has been great excitement— every one wanting it.

I suppose you remember, that Clarindy Hartman ran away to Desmoins about a year ago   Well she was married there a short time ago to a stage driver,— said to be a respectable man. I do not know his name. James Hartman has a daughter who was a week old last Wednesday;   they are very proud of her. Martin Hartman has got entirely well of his wound which they thought would prove fatal. Emily Pemberton was at the Newyear's ball, as well as every previous one with in the past year.[10] Her boy is a pretty, bright little fellow, and they seem very fond of him.

Your affectionate sister
Bella

Pa wishes you to read the article marked with a cross in the leaf of the Crisis, enclosed[11]

From Bella Williams

Homer Iowa Jan 15 1861

Dear James,

I received your letter yesterday. If you sent—or intended to send—Harpers Monthly regularly, I do not think we have received them all. It is truly a welcome visiter among us, but we are tempted to read at all times until it is exhausted, instead of keeping it to beguile the long winter evenings.— neglecting our work meanwhile are only slighting performing it. I pitty you, clogging through the streets in the wet— but more especially because of your business at such times;— for if it is as unpleasant to *give* as to receive such calls, I have some experience and can sympathiz with you.

I am sure I do not know whether we will stay here after next spring or not,— I think we will, for it seems as though Homer was our destiny so I try to put on a smiling face and be contented— but it is hard work some times. I do not think you need be fearful of coming in contact with "John Brownism" (by which I suppose you mean "abolitionism" and opposition to southern interests") for the praires which which— I didn't mean to write "which" twice—are our only companions are remarkably silent on the subject. and I will promise not to say a word on the subject, if you will only come home, and by the way. If you keep my mouth well stopped with novels, I believe I might consent to be come dum while you remained. Oh! ho, but the prarie chickens might croak abolitionism might they? Well, I shouldnt wonder! [12]

I am not surprised that you cannot bear to hear opinion expressed, opposite to your own; for it is the *inevitable result* of slavery. to produce a domineering spirit which is exercises against all who differ with its supporters; but oh me! oh me! you wont come home if I talk in this strain.

Altho' we differ so widly, your letters never jar our feelings very seriously, and at most provoke a smile and a musing "I wonder how he could have changed so."

By the way how came you to see any thing pritty in Lizzy. coming from the North as she did?
    "'Twas strange twas passing strange
        And wond'rous pitiful." [13]
But I dont mean the last line and wish I had not written it.

There is no sign of the snow going off yet and has lain a month.

I had a fine sleigh ride today to Bellville about seven miles distant [14]

Give my love to Lizzy and Love   Goodbye for tis late.
                                    Bella

I "shot off" a gun for the first time day before yesterday and
am quite proud of my exploit.

From Eleanor Williams

Dear James
We have received letters from you up to the 18 Jan.   they
are welcome visitors.   if a week passes without hearing from
you we are lonesome, and feel more and more anxious to have
you near enough to see you sometime.   in all our plans for
the future and castle building we have a plan for you and
Lizzy
Since your marriage we can think of you as not being a
stranger in a strange land but as haveing one fast friend, a
gentle hand to minister to you, a voice to council, a smiling
face to welcome you, how often do I picture to myself you sitting reading to her as you did to me in times past and wish I
could be one of the circle.   tell her we love her, because you
love her, and we have confidence in your choice. Tis your
wife and our daughter but we hope to see her and love her for
herself ere long.   we have shown the likeness to some of your
acquaintances   some say she is enough like you to be a sister   some that it is like Bella
This trouble between North and South makes us anxious.
when will it end? I do hope that we of the nineteenth century
can settle the difficulty with out resorting to arms   we are all
willing Uncle Sam should divide his estate if it is done peace-
ably   any thing but war   all we can do is to hope that those
in power will be of a quality that can be led by the Lord
to do what is just and right.   the most ultra men we have
among us are from the slave states[15]
This winter is severe   the snow is deep   the drifts around
the garden are as high as the fences so the cattle can walk
over   we will have trouble to save our trees   south and east
of us it has been deeper   the mails have been stopped.   it

rained all day yesterday and we were in hopes the snow would go off as the boys have not been able to get their fodder in from the farm on account of the depth of snow, but it is cold again to day and snow blowing

We received a letter from Grand Pa [Anderson] dated the 18th   he is in poor health. and says there is great excitement on account of the state of the country but here if we did not receive papers and news from you we would hear very little about it.[16]

We are all well   remember us to Lizzie

Your Mother

From Bella Williams

Homer Iowa February 15th, 1861

Dear James

I am happy as a lark this evening and as I have finished one garment to day and do not feel like commencing another, I think it an excellent opportunity to acknowledge the receipt of your letter of 28th ult. also, "Dickens' short stories," "Harper", and two "Frank Leslies"; for all of which you have my most cordial thanks— more particularly for the letter. I am much obliged to you for the correct orthography of "freeze". What a ridiculous mistake it was! I hope you wont spare me when I make such blunders in future.

I wish you would tell me the correct pronounciation of "A" in the numerous class of words of which the following are a few   Now, in "march", "parch", "starch", "father", etc it has the Italian or grave sound, and we pronounce it as "A" in "all", "fall" etc, only shorter and rather more obscure; while in "calm", "palm", "calf", etc, it has the same mark as in the forgoing list, and we pronounce it as in "man". Which is the right method? The more I pore over "Webster's Unabridged" the more mystified I get.

Pa, Rebecca, and I were at a dinner party in Webster City on 1st Jan at the residence of Lawyer [Jacob] Skinner, given in commemeration of our host's birthday. We are but slightly acquainted with the family having never seen Mrs [Polly] Skinner but once before[17]

She is a very pleasant and sociable lady but uneducated and introduced her guests—some twelve or fourteen in number all of whom were married—as "Mr and Miss" etc. which, as they were all strangers to us made it rather embarrassing. The eldest daughter at home is "Miss Nellie" about thirteen years of age. She* has two sisters and their families staying with them, and there were quite a number of little ladies and gentlemen who behaved in the best possible manner, and amused themselves waltzing while we dined.

Miss Nellie has a cousin about her own age but she was quite ill having taken a cold a few days before, and did not appear in the parlor.

They have a pianoforte and Nellie was finely prevailed upon to "play" for the benifit of the company notwithstanding she pleaded a "sore finger" as an excuse, but as Becky said, "the only wonder was that they were not all sore".   for she performed "Nellie Gray" and "We Met" in a stile that gave one some idea of the force and speed of the "Lightning train."   We passed a pleasant afternoon and rode home by starlight.

Rebecca has not entirely recovered from her disorder, but has frequent slight returns of it, at which times her left lower limb is swolen and painful. She seldom has roses in her cheeks, except when the frost bites them there, but then you know she never had, and, on the whole I think she is stronger than ever before.

We are all quiet here, but letters and papers are anxiously looked for and their contents eagerly devoured even by those who never manifested any interest in the afairs of the country before.

It is generally believed if war commences the Indians from a bove will be down upon us   if they *should* come I promise you I will do my best to "pop" a few of them, as George would say.

The weather is rather cold and the wind is "kettering' the

snow very much as it used to "in the good old times before you broke our family circle", but last Saturday and Sunday it rained, and of course settled the snow very much but only to make room for another, that came on Monday, and since then the wind has been busy pileing and repileing it and building all kinds of fantastic castles and fortifications arround our dwelings, and driving it through every crack and crivice and making minature Alps in our windowsills.

Give our love to Lizzie, and *take* it for yourself as a matter of course

Bella

By the way, James   I think the South ought to have more spirit than to send to the North for Military goods or indeed for anything els.[18]

It is rumored that the capture of Ft. Pickens has been given up as a hopeless undertaking   is it true?[19]

Bella

*I mean *Mrs.* Skinner, not Miss Nellie

From Bella Williams

Homer Hamilton Co Iowa February 27 1861

Dear James

Yours to Becky, and third inst. was received day before yesterday;   we are in excellent spirits at the bare possibility of seeing you and Lizzie, at some future period, tho' it may befar diste[n]t   We are also very much gratified to know you cherish the memory of this poor little white cottage with "its lean-to and stove pipe" and I assure you it is not changed much— at least, not for the better.

I am sorry to say we have not,—I mean *Becky* has not— received [Dickens'] "Nicholas Nickleby" as yet but I have again to thank you for a "Frank Leslie", "New York Illustrated news" and the "St. Clairsville [Ohio] Gazette and Citizen".

The Gentleman whom Miss [Elizabeth B.] Smith married is a widdower with two grown up daughters, a son fifteen years of age, and a little daughter, aged eight years. They reside in Chicago. So much for *that* bundle of affectation and conceit![20]

We have had four warm days, in succession and the snow is rappidly disappearing, but we are daily expecting it to "wind up" with an other snow storm.

Tho' we are so anxious to see you, I would almost be sorry to have you come West to live, for altho we can bear the hardships and privations I feel that I would not want Lizzie and you to try them.

I am ashamed of this—as well I may be—but I am in a hurry, and perhaps it will be better than not to hear from us at all.

Miss Maria Bromby was married a short time ago to Mr Melrose of Goldfield Wright Co Iowa

Bella

From J. H. Williams

Homer Hamilton Co Iowa March 10 1861

Dear James

When I wrote last I intended to write again in a few days but the same procrastinating spirit which led me to put off writing on the subject of your marriage for months previous to its occurence, has kept me from alluding to it till now. The reluctance for I felt it as such— has not arrisen from indifference, but from the importance of the step you were about to take and now have taken   having no knowledge of "Lizy" I did not feel at liberty to risk any advice in the premises. But now that your election is made "and *that it is all over*"— that serious views of life must if ever begin to be entertaind and knowing no reason why "Lizy" should not be numberd among the objects of immediate affection, and welcomed to our humble domestic circle this *reluctant-restraint* has passed away

My dear children, I trust you will constantly look to the Lord to direct your every step in life— So shall the true ends of Marriage be attained— *Happiness in this life Fitness* for *Heaven*— and a *spiritual-union* which is to be *Eternal*.

There are three great epochs in human life— *Birth Marriage*, and *Death*! The first commences or introduces as a state of *endless-being*— The 2nd more than tinges, it *determines* in a great degree the quality of the man, while the 3rd ushers in the final state of happiness, or *woe* which life has fited us for enjoying! Every particular of the Devine providence is to fit us for, and draw us to *heaven*; and as the Kingdom of god must be formed within before it can be enjoyed, and this can be done only in the excercise of our reason, and liberty we may invest, or pervert the whole, and be unhappy! *Marriage itself*, the great instrument for humanising and drawing us out of the Love of our selves into the love of *Others*, and into Supreme *Love* to God and as a consequence into the enjoyment of heavenly happiness may be turned into the procureing cause of the greatest misery here and here after. We are born Sensual, that is we are influenced by the senses only. By the acquirement of knowledge we rise to the natural state into which the Brute is born, but if we stop with a Knowledge of natural things and a desire to posess them we halt in the middle of the course intended for us and in no ways surpass the "beasts that perish", except in duration   Now as we become rational in natural things by acquireing a knowledge of them, and of their uses, so we become rational in heavenly things by acquireing a knowledge of spiritual things.   when we apply this knowledge to the regulation of our conduct, Which will lead us to clearer views of our spiritual constitution and wants, and make us truly wise! The wisdom thus acquired, is not "*fossilized*" but eternally progressive

I intended to write you a series of letters in refference to Marriage— and its instrumentality in opening in our minds all the fountains of heavenly beatitutde not in this life only but more fully in the next. Indeed in this life internal and surrounding evils have such power that the scene at best is checkered with disappointments trials & sufferings of varied form! These sorrows & chastisements are necessary to drag into light closely in hereing evils which otherwise could not be seen much less be acknowledged and put away as sins against *God*! But instead of these letters I have concluded my purpose will be better attained by sending you a book which is mailed with this letter. I hope you will both study it carefully, and may the Lord bless you with that wisdom which can be obtained from him alone who is the *Light* and *Life* of *the world*

We are looking now with anxiety for the presidents inaugural to see whether it breaths peace or war and strange to tell, many are anxious for the latter   I hope he will see it is now too late— that cession [secession] belongs to the past, for which he is not responsible but I fear that madness will rule the hour!— [21]   We have had a great amount of snow. As much as in [18]56−7 but not so cold as that year tho cold enough. Was glad to see the Statement of the tempreture in Mobile for several years.   Changes in warm climates seem harder to beare than in cold. Forest trees are not killed or split by 30 to 40 degrees below zero, nor are hens frozen on the nest in anything deserving the name of a henhouse in this latitude much as the winds often aid in removeing the animal heat.

The spring opens promiseing   More so than it was thot it would   The snow drifts were so deep

As to the matter nearest to my own heart as well as that of all I am at loss to know what to say. I refer to your coming home. There is land enough to operate on, and there is no doubt about makeing a successful liveing and more too if it is desired   nor would the attention be greater than is necessary in any other business while the irksome and unhealthy confinements is wholy dispensed with, nor need the labor be hard if rightly managed   What then is in the way? There is industry wanted which is wanted in every other employment.

There is some capital or patience & economy in its stead and last but not the least by far, there is union of effort wanted farming requires the attention of several who will take the right kind of interest— devide the labor & care, and at times manage different parts of the operation. I need this spring some one fit to go to market with the stock (as I must sell and pay off) while there should be those left in charge of home operations who had more *experience* and *push* than can be expected of *boys*

I have concluded not to send the Book Conjugial-Love till I hear from you again as I doubt somewhat the postal arrangements in the present state of things

We think times begin to look more encouraging here. Not that money is much plentier. But people are farming better, and those who will pay are geting out of debt, and we are geting [used?] to it. The rapidly increaseing population of the northwest Must soon raise land here. In this view of the subject I would like to see you here. If we did not like it, we could sell in a short time and have the means of going elsewhere.

Your affectionate father
J. H. Williams

From Rebecca & Bella Williams

Homer Hamilton Co Iowa March 25 1861

Dear James,

How would you like to call Bella "school marm". She commenced teaching Monday. had 19 scholars the first day and 25 the last of the weeke.

The snow went off in a hurry when it got started and it is drying up very fast now though it has been pretty cold for a few days. Bella got a letter from Francis dated Mar 6th she says the violets were in bloom. They are a head of us.

I wish you would come back soon but I am getting tired of waiting on you.

Pa does not know whether he will farm mutch this year or
not   he talks of renting some of the land and if he does he
and John will only put in a little wheat and let Parker go to
school. All well

Your affectionate sister,
Becky

Tell Lizzie I have received her beautiful present and fully ap-
preciate it as well as her disinterestedness in sending me the
prettiest though you advised her to keep it for her self.   You
naughty boy!   you thought I would be just as well satisfied
because I would not know any thing about the other?   Very
true, but it is equally true that I would rather have Lizzie's
gift than the gold belt *you* sent me.

Thank you very much for the copy slips.—   they came the
same day I got my certificate from Mr. Blair,— though I suppose you intended them for my use,— and I will use them.   I
have engaged to teach a quarter for forty dollars.

Yours in great haste
Bella

Becky has received a Harper['s *Weekly*] Pa a letter, and I a
[Godey's] Lady's book [a] Frank Leslie and quite a number
of Mobile papers have also "come in hand", for all of which
you have our thanks. Please over look and excuse my last
letter, I was in a bad humor— which I am sorry to say is frequently the case— when I wrote it.

Epilogue

John H. Williams survived the economic woes of the 1850s and lived in Hamilton County for the balance of his life. He continued to be very diligent in New Church activities on the frontier. In a report to the Illinois Association in October 1864, he noted that "Our members have formed themselves into a society . . . of eleven adult members." The whole number of baptisms was thirty-one. He preached in the schoolhouse every sabbath and the sabbath school was "attended by a number on the outside of the church." "So is the preaching," he added. The following year, he reported that he had officiated at two weddings and one funeral and baptised four people, three of whom were infants. He was also very "anxious to enter the missionary field in Iowa," but had "not been able to make the arrangements." In October 1866 he wrote that there were thirteen adults in the society and that the sabbath school had "an interesting, though small library." During the year he had officiated at three funerals, preached every other sabbath, and given "several discourses in the country." In the 1870 census his occupation is listed as farmer for the first and last time. He reported the value of his real estate as $7,000 and of his personal property as $700. Becky, Bella, and George were still living at home. In the mid-seventies, he became seriously and painfully ill. He died at the age of seventy-five on September 26, 1880, at the state sanitarium in Independence, Iowa. On October 6, 1880, the editor of the *Hamilton Freeman*, in noting his recent death, commented: "J. H. Williams, a former well-known and highly esteemed citizen of Homer . . . was a man of culture and ability and his fate has been a matter of deep concern to his intelligent and worthy family."[1] His obituary in the *New Jerusalem Messenger* noted that "his disease was cancer of the head, causing great suffering, both mental and physical, for the last five years." "Mr. Williams," it continued, "was endowed with great intellectual capacities, and being full of love for truth acquired, and possessing a fitness for presenting the same to others, he seemed to be a power in the pulput. [In Iowa] he traveled with his own conveyance, preaching, selling and distributing New Church books, without receiving scarcely any pecuniary aid. Thus he spent his talents, time and means in spreading the truth until checked by failing health."[2]

Eleanor Frances Williams continued to live in Hamilton County for a number of years after her husband's death. She died on May 24, 1891, at the age of seventy-six while visiting Bella in Saguache, Colorado.[3]

Hugh Anderson died on May 20, 1866, in his eighty-fifth year. The editor of the St. Clairsville (Ohio) *Gazette* described him as "a very intelligent and much esteemed citizen. . . . He continued to wield the burin with unabated skill to the last, and left a map of Athens County unfinished. Among his later works is a large map containing both the ancient and modern names of places—the historical designs of T. Genin—several County maps—and a map of Ohio. He was distinguished for minding his own business—punctuality—and patient investigation."

Soon after the Civil War began, James enlisted in the Twenty-first Alabama Infantry, Volunteers. He led his company at the battle of Shiloh in April 1862, where he was cited for gallantry. The regiment was then ordered to the Mobile area for the balance of the war. By June 1863, James had been promoted to lieutenant colonel. He commanded one small battery, Fort Powell, in the battle of Mobile Bay in August 1864 and was the regimental commander during the last few months of the war. In the years after the war, as his family grew (he and his wife had two sons and three daughters, one of whom was named Eleanor Frances), he served as a clerk, first for the Mobile and Ohio Railroad and later for the Mobile County probate court. He helped found and was active in veterans' organizations for over three decades. He also participated in civic, social, and cultural organizations. When he died in 1903 after an extended illness not unlike his father's, the editor of the Mobile *Daily Register* wrote: "James M. Williams who died yesterday was a courageous and ready soldier, a patriotic and earnest citizen and an honest man, a gentleman, in the fullest sense of the word. It would be well for the republic if every man were to mold his life to conform to the high ideals that inspired our friend who has gone to the other world."[4]

Mary Rebecca, despite her early childhood illness, lived a long life. She lived with her parents for a number of years after the war and taught school at Homer and other rural schools in the southwestern part of the county. Her obituary, in the Webster City *Daily Freeman-Journal* began with the headline: "'Aunt Beckey' Williams Dead," and continued, "Aunt Beckey was loved by the earlier residents of the Homer community for her work among the children in the rural schools. She was a typical pioneer woman, very active in the social and public life of her community. Naturally very energetic and possessed of a high order of ability, she was an outstanding woman for many years in the pioneer section of the county where most of her activities lay." She married the Rev. William K. S. Hillhouse rather late in life, and they moved to New York State and later to Oklahoma. After her husband's death in 1906, she continued to teach. Later she tutored children in New York. In the late 1920s, she returned to the Duncombe area and lived comfortably with her nephew, James Frank Williams. While visiting a niece in Whittier, California, in 1931 she became ill and, after an extended illness, died on July 18, 1933, at the age of eighty-three. She was buried in the Webster City cemetery.[5]

Isabella also lived with her parents for a number of years. In the 1870 census she is listed as being in the millinery business. Like Becky, she married late in life. She met and married George W. Beckley in Saguache, Colorado, probably while visiting her brother John, and they had a mercantile store for many years. She died in 1918.[6]

John, Jr., who disliked school so much, had a long career in government service. He freighted across the plains with ox teams to Colorado in 1861. Upon returning, he enlisted in Company G of the First Iowa Cavalry and served in the western theater until discharged as a sergeant in 1865. After farming in the Homer area for a few years, he married Elizabeth Shoults and they moved to Saguache, Colorado, to improve his health. The climate must have agreed with him; they had eleven children and he had a long life. He became active in Republican party politics and was soon appointed deputy county clerk. He held the position until 1880, when he was appointed county commissioner. He also served two terms as county judge and two as county commissioner by election. From 1898 until 1913 he served as postmaster of Saguache. All this time he was also in the hardware business and ranching. After he retired, they moved to Moab, Utah, then to Grand Junction, Colorado, and finally, in 1915, to nearby Fruita. He lived there until his death on May 3, 1933, at the age of ninety.[7]

Joseph Parker Williams, although only fifteen, joined his brother John in Company G of the First Iowa Cavalry in November 1864 and served until November 1865. He was in poor health for the balance of his life. In the 1870 census he is listed as a jeweller in the Homer area. By 1883 he had moved to Demopolis, Alabama. He married a woman named Maggie and they had three children. The family later moved to Laurel, Mississippi, where he died on February 6, 1891.[8]

George Hite Williams was the only child to remain in the area. His farm was two and one-half miles west of Homer. In 1871 he married Harriet Brewer, and they had two sons and two daughters. He moved to Fort Dodge in 1903, where he was secretary of the Farmers' Mutual Insurance Company until his death on January 4, 1921.[9]

In May 1865 the Chicago and Northwestern Railway was completed to Boone. This attracted settlers into the area, and for the next five years Homer enjoyed a boomlet. The range of prices of lots in town increased from $10−15 to $50−75, and the usual businesses began to appear. However, with the completion of the railroad to Webster City in 1870, a Hamilton County history noted, "the decline of the town was as rapid as the growth had been."[10] According to the census of 1910, there were two merchants and one small farm equipment dealer in Webster Township. The post office was discontinued on September 30, 1913. As of 1983, the only indication of its former existence was the Homer Methodist Church and a farm implement store with the name Homer on a small sign in front.

Notes

Some of the notes given below contain biographical information from the 1860 federal population census expressed in a standard format: husband's name, occupation, age, wealth (real estate first, then personal estate), place of birth; wife's data; number of children and range of their ages. An example of this format can be found in the notes for chapter 1, note 4.

Introduction

1. From James Williams's obituary in the St. Clairsville (Ohio) *Gazette,* Feb. 11, 1903.
2. Early biographical data for John Hugh Williams and Hugh Anderson were furnished by Williams's granddaughter, Doris Williams Ekstrom, of Duncombe, Iowa. See Williams's advertisements in the St. Clairsville (Ohio) *Gazette,* from 1838 to 1852, especially Feb. 28, 1847, and Jan. 15, 1852. Anderson's obituary is in the June 7, 1866, issue. Information on the Williamses' activities in the New Church is from the *Journal of the Fourteenth Annual Meeting of the New Church Western Convention, Held In Cincinnati, May 21, 1846,* 6; *Journal of the Fifteenth Annual Meeting of the New Church Western Convention, Held in Cincinnati, May 20, 1847,* 7; *Journal of the Sixteenth Annual Meeting of the New Church Western Convention, Held in Cincinnati, May 17, 1848,* 1, 23–25 (all of the New Church proceedings were printed by Otis Clapp of Boston); *Journal of the Proceedings of the New Church, Held in Cincinnati, From Friday the 18th to Sunday the 20th of May, 1849,* 9; *Journal of the Second Annual Meeting of the Ohio Association; Held in Cincinnati, May 17, 1850,* 28–29; *Minutes of the First Meeting of the Ohio Conference of the New Church, Held in Cincinnati, Ohio, on Saturday and Sunday, May 22 and 23, 1852,*

(Boston: Otis Clapp, 1852), 2–8, 32–36; *Journal of the Proceedings of the Thirty-fourth General Convention of the New Church in the United States* (Boston: Otis Clapp, 1852), 75; Ophia D. Smith, "The New Jerusalem Church in Ohio from 1848 to 1870," *Ohio State Archaeological and Historical Journal* 62 (Jan. 1953): 27. Born in Ireland in 1782, Anderson emigrated to Philadelphia in 1809, where he became a well-known engraver. By 1820 he was associated with F. Lucas, Jr., in Baltimore. In about 1826 he moved to Cadiz, Ohio, and subsequently to St. Clairsville, where he continued his business. He engraved a large portion of the plates of the American edition of the *Edinburgh Encyclopedia,* as well as many historical and Ohio county maps. He was also active in Belmont County, Ohio, Democratic party politics during the 1830s and 1840s. John Kent Folmar, ed., "Pre–Civil War Sentiment from Belmont County: Correspondence of Hugh Anderson," *Ohio History* 78 (Summer 1969): 202–3, 209; Paul E. Rieger, Sylvania, Ohio, letter to editor, Nov. 19, 1969.

Emmanuel Swedenborg (1688–1771), a Swedish scholar, politician, and theologian, published some thirty works on cosmology and the nature of the human soul. He taught that eternal life is an inner condition beginning with earthly life, that the progression of man's spirit is through selflessness, and that "Love is the life of man." Shortly after his death, reading groups were established in London and Philadelphia. Although never a major denomination, the Church of New Jerusalem gained considerable attention during the nineteenth century. Eric A. Sutton, *The Living Thoughts of Swedenborg* (London: Cassell and Co., 1947), 14–15.

3. Williams's store was apparently located on Lot 1, on the corner of Third and Washington streets. The lots cost $760. Iowa, Hamilton County, Town Lot Deed Book 1, pp. 121–22, 210, Recorders Office, Hamilton County Courthouse, Webster City.

4. The original Webster County had formerly been Risley and Yell counties. Homer, in Webster Township, was surveyed and laid out in the fall of 1853 in the southwestern quarter of section 6, township 87N, range 26W. The original plan was six squares by seven, with eight lots per square. In January 1855 the Snell and Butterworth Addition added eighteen squares. The lots were 132 feet by 70⅛ feet, the streets were 66 feet

wide, and the alleys 16½ feet wide. Iowa, Hamilton County, Deed Book of Plats 1, p. 60, Recorders Office, Hamilton County Courthouse, Webster City; *The census returns of the different counties of the state of Iowa in 1856,* . . . (Iowa City, Ia.: Crum & Boyce, 1857), unpaged; Jacob A. Swisher, "The Location of County Seats in Iowa," *Iowa Journal of History and Politics* 22 (April, July, 1924): 249, 356; J. W. Lee, *History of Hamilton County,* Iowa (Chicago: S. J. Clarke Co., 1912), 1: 59–60; Bessie L. Lyon, "The Passing of Homer," *The Palimpsest* 3 (Dec. 1922): 381–89; "John F. Duncombe's 1856 Journal," Ft. Dodge *Messenger,* Nov. 23, 1983; "Homer, the First County Seat," Ft. Dodge *Messenger and Chronicle,* Aug. 31, 1935; W. Oakley Ruggles, "Early Recollections of Fort Dodge," *Iowa Journal of History* 49 (April 1951): 170–75; Bessie L. Lyon, *Early Days In Hamilton County* (Webster City, Ia.: Freeman-Journal Publishing Co., 1946), 18–19, 56–59; *General Meeting of Receivers of the Heavenly Doctrines of the New Jerusalem, Held at Urbana, Ohio, Jan. 4–6, 1856* (Boston: Otis Clapp, 1855), 7.

5. John H. Williams wrote thirty-one letters that have survived; Eleanor, his wife, thirteen; Isabella, seventeen; Mary Rebecca, eight; George Hite, four; and Joseph Parker, two. One letter has also survived from James's friend Columbus Pemberton.

6. Lewis E. Atherton, *The Pioneer Merchant in Mid-America* (Columbia: University of Missouri Press, 1939), 43.

7. Allan G. Bogue, *From Prairie to Corn Belt: Farming on the Illinois and Iowa Prairies in the Nineteenth Century* (Chicago: University of Chicago Press, 1963), 196.

8. Allan G. Bogue, "Pioneer Farmers and Innovation," *Iowa Journal of History* 56 (Jan. 1958): 4.

9. John Kent Folmar, ed., *From That Terrible Field: Civil War Letters of James M. Williams, Twenty-first Alabama Infantry Volunteers* (Tuscaloosa: University of Alabama Press, 1981).

1. "Iowa never looked more delightful"

1. Eleanor, 45. Nine-year-old Rebecca had a seriously abscessed abdomen.

2. On April 2, 1855, Williams sold 208 acres of land in Ohio

to one Jacob Long for $4,000; Ohio, Belmont County, Deed Book 39, p. 456, Belmont County Courthouse, St. Clairsville, Ohio. Long's inability or refusal to pay and the litigation that followed were continuing economic burdens for the family.

3. Bella was thirteen years of age.

4. Twelve-year-old John Dally was one of ten children. Milton, farmer, 41, $800, $300, Ohio; Margaret, 41, Ohio; the children were age 21 to six months.

5. Church, hotel keeper, 32, $2,000, $300, Ohio; Jane, 28; three children ages 9 to 2 months. A veteran of the Mexican War, he was elected constable of Webster Township in October 1859; Webster City *Hamilton Freeman,* Oct. 22, 1859.

6. Pemberton, carpenter, 52, $300 (personal), Va.; C. C., 49; five children, ages 21 to 3. He was the secretary of the Republican party's county committee; Webster City *Hamilton Freeman,* Oct. 8, 1858. Chancy, laborer, 28, Ohio; Mary, 27; one child, age 2.

7. The sorghum cane, grown to make molasses, was not a successful experiment. See Bella's letter of November 7, 1858.

8. McPheeters, farmer, 31, $3,000, $1,000, Ind.; Elizabeth, 24, Ill.; two young children. He was the justice of the peace and the Ft. Dodge *Sentinel*'s agent in Homer; Ft. Dodge *Sentinel,* October 23, 1858.

9. Prairie Creek originates near the old Homer cemetery about one-half mile east of Homer and flows south into the Boone River.

10. Fisher, clerk, 28, $600 (real), Ind.; J. A., 23, Ill.

11. Mrs. Porterfield, 32, Ohio; James, farmer, 35, $100 (personal); daughter, age 2.

12. Congressional candidates William Vandever, a Republican from Dubuque, and W. F. Leffingwell, a Democrat, debated in Union Hall in Webster City on the evening of August 18. The Second District consisted of most of the northern half of Iowa. Vandever won a seat to the Thirty-sixth Congress in the October election, was reelected in 1860, and served until September 1861, when he was mustered into service as a colonel in the Ninth Iowa Infantry Regiment. Promoted to brigadier general in 1862, he led a brigade for most of the balance of the war. Webster City *Hamilton Freeman,* Aug. 20, 1858; Ezra J. Warner, *Generals in Blue: Lives of Union Commanders* (Baton

Rouge: Louisiana State University Press, 1964), 523–24. The Webster City newspaper was established on June 20, 1857. The masthead emphasized its support for the "free soil, free labor, freeman" Republican party.

13. Hartman, carpenter, 39, $500, $100, Va.; Elvira, 35, five children, ages 8 to 2.

14. Daniels, lawyer, 41, $2,000, $500, Pa.; five children, ages 17 to 3.

15. Swanger, farmer, 22, Ohio. Drisilla lived in Church's hotel.

16. Sereptha Tucker, who was sixteen in 1858, soon married a merchant named Butterworth, who lived in Webster Township, Webster County. He listed $35,000 in real property and $50,000 in personal property in the 1860 census. Their marriage is referred to in Bella's letter of November 7, 1858.

17. A melodeon is a small reed organ.

18. This is the only existing nonfamily letter written to James. Columbus, H. C. Pemberton's son, soon died of consumption.

19. The eighty-acre farm, located in the eastern half of section 21, was about halfway to Webster City; Iowa, Hamilton County, Deed Book 1, pp. 297–98.

20. Mrs. Smith, 52, N.J.; J. S., lawyer, 54, $300 (personal).

21. J. H. Williams had made a trip back to Ohio since moving to Iowa.

22. He was also the president of the school board.

23. Phrenology is the psychological or analytical method based on the idea that certain mental faculties and character traits are indicated by the configuration of the skull.

24. John Hugh Williams, Jr., was fifteen years of age.

25. Blair, farmer, 31, $3,000, $200, N.Y.; Ellen A., 22. In October 1859 he was elected county superintendent of schools; Webster City *Hamilton Freeman*, Oct. 22, 1859.

26. Brown, merchant, 43, St. Clairsville, Ohio.

27. Gregory and Messemore, merchants, began advertising their products in the Ft. Dodge *Sentinel* on January 12, 1859.

28. Brushy Creek is about four miles west of Homer in Webster County. It flows south into the Des Moines River.

29. Emma, 19, Illinois.

30. A French leave is a sudden departure without notice.

31. "Jakne" was probably Emma's eleven-year-old brother, J. W. Pemberton.

32. Oscar J. Daniels, fifteen, was the lawyer's eldest son. George Hite Williams was almost eight years of age.
33. Cowan, lawyer, 34, St. Clairsville, Ohio.
34. The "Pikes Peak or Bust" gold rush of 1858–59 attracted national attention, particularly because of the hard times. See LeRoy R. Hafen, *Colorado: The Story of a Western Commonwealth* (1933; reprint, New York: AMS, 1970), 105–8. On March 26, 1859, the *Hamilton Freeman* reported that "The Pike's Peak fever has about dried up in this vicinity. . . . The late discouraging accounts have dampened the ardor of our heretofore enthusiastic Pike's Peakers."
35. To "see the elephant" meant "to go to town, maybe for the first time; to see the world and gain experience of its sin and glitter, generally at some cost to the investigator" (Peter Watts, *Dictionary of the Old West* [New York: Alfred A. Knopf, 1977], 125).
36. This is the first reference, and it is only an allusion, by any member of the family to the increasingly bitter sectional controversy after the passage in 1854 of the Kansas-Nebraska Act, which provided for "popular sovereignty" on the slavery question. The act led to the formation of the Republican party, which was opposed to the expansion of slavery, and to the emergence of two factions, one proslavery and one antislavery, in Kansas. Shannon was the controversial second governor of Kansas Territory from September 1855 until August 1856, during which time "Bleeding Kansas" became a national political issue. William Frank Zornow, *Kansas: A History of the Jayhawk State* (Norman: University of Oklahoma Press, 1957), 68–74. The John Dally referred to in this section may be the father of the twelve-year-old boy named John Dalley referred to in Eleanor Williams' letter of August 19, 1858. The father's name is indistinct in the 1860 census manuscript schedule.
37. Daniels owned a general supply store in Iowa City "opposite the Crummy House," as advertised in the *Hamilton Freeman* during June and July, 1858.
38. Williams apparently had considered moving to Urbana, Ohio, prior to the Iowa decision.
39. On April 16, 1859, the *Hamilton Freeman* reported that the "Steamboat Charles Rogers came up [the Des Moines River] to Ft. Dodge one day last week. The Ft. Dodgers were elated. . . . We trust . . . this enterprise may prove eminently suc-

cessful." On May 28, the editor wondered whether the Boone River might not be navigable despite the presence of a number of mill dams.

40. Swede Point was located about twelve miles south of Homer.

41. This comment by Bella is the first reaction to James's gradual conversion to the Southern way of life.

42. Spirit Lake, north of Ft. Dodge near the Minnesota boundary, was the site of the Spirit Lake massacre of 1857. Church was also first lieutenant of the militia company, the Frontier Guard, that had recently returned from the Spirit Lake area, where it had been sent in reaction to rumors of another uprising. Leland L. Sage, *A History of Iowa* (Ames: Iowa State University Press, 1974), 107; "John F. Duncombe's 1856 Journal," Ft. Dodge *Messenger*, Nov. 23, 24, 1983; Webster City *Hamilton Freeman*, Jan. 7, 1859.

43. Dally, farmer, 73, $400, $300, Pa.; Margaret, 62. The references to "paper" and "broken Bank bills" are to bank notes or bills of exchange. Those stolen from Williams were from failed, or broken, banks and were thus worthless.

2. "Lessons of humility and of humanity"

1. Parker Anderson, farmer, 36, $100, $500; Martha, 28; four children, ages 6 to infancy. Parker was Eleanor's brother.

2. Miller, farmer, 33, $640 (real), Pa. He died of pleurisy in early 1861; Webster City *Hamilton Freeman*, Feb. 2, 1861.

3. Corbin, physician, 39, $6,960, $1,200, Pa.; Maria, 37; six children, ages 13 to 1. Corbin, Homer's first physician, had moved to Webster City by this time. In 1859 he was elected county judge. Lee, *History of Hamilton County*, 1:111.

4. Joseph Parker Williams was eleven years of age.

5. The two letters J. H. Williams mentions are missing.

6. Fisher, clerk, 28, $600 (real), Ind.; S. A., 24, Ill.

7. Rev. Samuel Noble, *An Appeal in Behalf of the Views of the Eternal World and State and the Doctrines of Faith and Life Held by the body of Christians who believe that a New Church is signified in the Revelation, . . . by The New Jerusalem. . . .* (London: J. S. Hodson, 1826). This publication was an important doctrinal explanation and defense of Swedenborg's writings.

8. Maxwell, farmer, 51, $4,000, $300, Va.; four children, ages 18 to 8. He was elected the first county judge in August 1857, when he defeated A. Moon by fourteen votes (172 to 158); Webster City *Hamilton Freeman*, Aug. 6, 1857; A. T. Andreas, *Illustrated Historical Atlas of the State of Iowa* (Chicago: Andreas Atlas Co., 1875), 459.

9. The schottische is a round dance resembling the polka.

10. Mrs. DeWitt, 43, Pa.; Barnabas, tailor, 43, $400 (real); three children, ages 12 to 9.

11. Wolsey, farmer, 38, $1,000, $1,100, Ohio; Jeanette, 37; seven children, ages, 16 to 1. They lived in Webster Township, Webster County, just across the county line from Homer.

12. Border Plains was a village in Webster County on the road from Homer to Ft. Dodge and about three miles north of present-day Lehigh. Located in the center of the county, it was a convenient meeting place in the early years. The schoolhouse located there was donated by Evon and Doris Ekstrom to the Ft. Dodge Historical Museum in 1964.

13. Boonesboro, now part of Boone, was about thirty miles south of Homer.

14. Rachel, a cousin, lived at 1204 Locust St. in Philadelphia. She taught school and often wrote to James.

15. Gravel was a condition similar to kidney stones.

16. Hall, farmer, 39, Vt.; Charlotte, 21, Ohio.

17. Sibert, farmer, 38, $400, $100, Pa.; Elizabeth, 24, Ohio; four children, ages 6 to infancy.

18. This is the first reference to the presidential election year of 1860. The Republican party nominated Abraham Lincoln in Chicago on May 18. The Democratic party, torn by the sectional dispute and unable to select a presidential candidate, had adjourned on May 3 in Charleston, South Carolina. The northern wing met in Baltimore on June 18 and chose Stephen A. Douglas as its nominee.

    James apparently did not tell his family that he had become interested in the military and that he had joined a local militia company, the Clinch Rifles.

19. Rachel, 12, and George DeWitt, 9, Pa., Barnabas' children. Corbin, farmer, 21, $150 (personal), Ohio; Muhala, 20.

20. Wolsey's Grove was about three-fourths of a mile west of Homer in Webster Township, Webster County.

21. U.S. Bureau of the Census, Manuscript Census of Population, Hamilton and Webster Counties, Iowa, 1860.

3. "The storm that hovers on the horizon"

1. George, J. H. Williams's brother, lived near Bowling Green in Wood County, Ohio. He and his family were also New Churchmen. *Journal of Proceedings of the Ohio Association. August 29, 1856. Second Annual New Church Meeting of Ohio* (Boston: Otis Clapp, 1856), 26.
2. Imphee is an African sorghum.
3. The statue commemorating Oliver Hazard Perry's victory on Lake Erie was unveiled and dedicated on September 10, 1860. It was the forty-seventh anniversary of the event.
4. Miller, carpenter, 29, Ohio; Ann, 28; two daughters, 7 and 3.
5. Unknown to his family, James had fallen in love with Eliza Jane Rennison, a seventeen-year-old Augusta belle. Also, he had decided to take a new job in Mobile, Alabama, as a bookkeeper for James Conning, a nationally known manufacturer of silver, jewelry, and swords. On November 12 he left Augusta for his new job. Three weeks later he returned and married "Lizzy." Folmar, *From That Terrible Field*, p. xi.
6. Marshalltown, in Marshall County, is about sixty-five miles southeast of Homer.
7. Lincoln had been elected president on November 6, yet no one in the family had commented upon that fact. The unofficial presidential election returns for Hamilton County were: Lincoln, 234; Douglas, 100; John C. Breckenridge (the Southern Democratic candidate), 13. Webster City *Hamilton Freeman*, Nov. 7, 1860.
8. The underground railroad was a clandestine effort by black and white abolitionists and humanitarians to help fugitive slaves escape into the north and on to Canada. There were "secret agents" and "stations" along the various routes. For the mythology of the underground railroad, see Larry Gara, *The Liberty Line: The Legend of the Underground Railroad* (Lexington: University of Kentucky Press, 1961), 1–18.
9. Alexander H. Stephens, first a Whig and later a Democratic

representative from 1843 to 1859, had been asked by the legislature to comment on the sectional crisis. In a widely circulated letter to the Georgia legislature of November 14, 1860, he opposed secession and suggested that Lincoln's election was no reason for hasty action. He preferred a regional convention instead. After Georgia's secession, however, he helped organize the Confederacy and became its controversial vice-president.

10. Emily, 19, Ill. She was Columbus's sister.

11. The periodical titled *Crisis: A New Church Weekly and Family Periodical* was a Swedenborgian journal published in LaPorte, Indiana.

12. By this date, South Carolina, Mississippi, Florida, and Alabama had seceded from the Union. John Brown, an extreme abolitionist, led the raid on the federal arsenal at Harper's Ferry, Virginia, on October 16, 1859, for which he and six of his followers were hanged. The incident greatly exacerbated sectional tensions.

13. Lizzy's family was from Newburgh, New York. The quote is from Shakespeare's *Othello*, act 1, scene 3, line 160.

14. Bellville was south of Homer on the Boone River.

15. Delegates from six states met in Montgomery, Alabama, on February 4 and soon established the provisional Confederate States of America.

16. On January 18, Grandpa Anderson wrote to James that "Its indeed a matter of regret that the U.S. union should be disolved. I blame the fanatics of the North, and regret that I am living among them" (Folmar, "Pre–Civil War Sentiment in Belmont County," 208).

17. Skinner, farmer, 50, $2,000, $2,500, N.Y.; Polly, 43, Pa.

18. President Buchanan's controversial secretary of war, John T. Floyd, had allowed the shipment of weapons to the Southern states in December and January. There were charges in the North that he had intentionally allowed these sales during the secession crisis. These charges have been discredited. James G. Randall and David Donald, *The Civil War and Reconstruction* (Lexington, Mass.: D. C. Heath and Co., 1969), 310–11.

19. As the Deep South states seceded, their troops seized most of the federal forts and arsenals. Located on the eastern tip of Santa Rosa Island, Ft. Pickens protected the excellent harbor at Pensacola, Florida. The fort was not captured by the Confederates.

20. Miss Smith was from Fort Dodge. She married N. S. Cushing, who lived in Chicago. Unidentified newspaper clipping, Williams Collection.
21. Lincoln was inaugurated on March 4, 1861, six days prior to this letter.

Epilogue

1. "Journal of the Twenty-Fifth Annual Meeting of the Illinois Association of the New Jerusalem, held at the Temple in Peoria, on the 7th, 8th, and 9th days of October, 1864," *The New Jerusalem Magazine* 37 (1864–65), 16; "Journal of the Twenty-Sixth Annual Meeting of the Illinois Association of the New Jerusalem, held in the Temple in Chicago, on the 6th, 7th, and 8th days of October, 1865," *The New Jerusalem Magazine* 38 (1865–66), 11–12; "Journal of the Annual Meeting of the Illinois Association of the New Jerusalem, held in the Temple in Canton, on the 19th, 20th, and 21st days of October, 1866," *The New Jerusalem Magazine* 39 (1866–67), 12.
2. *New Jerusalem Messenger*, Nov. 24, 1880, p. 318. For Williams's death certificate, see Iowa, Dept. of Health, Vital Records Section, Certification of Death No. 10-80-78, Des Moines, Iowa.
3. Irene Williams Marold, Saguache, Colorado, interview with editor, Feb. 9, 1983. Mrs. Marold is the granddaughter of John H. Williams, Jr. On her tombstone Mrs. Williams's name is spelled "Ellinor."
4. Folmar, *From That Terrible Field*, xiii–xvi.
5. Webster City *Daily Freeman-Journal*, July 21, 1933.
6. Marold interview.
7. *Progressive Men of Western Colorado* (Chicago: A. W. Bowen & Co., 1905), 812–13; undated newspaper obituary, Williams Collection.
8. National Archives, Pension Records, Pension Application File 482846; U. S. Bureau of the Census, Manuscript Census of Population, Webster Township, Webster County, Iowa, 1870.
9. Doris Williams Ekstrom, Duncombe, Iowa, interview with editor, Feb. 1, 1983; undated newspaper obituary, Williams Collection.
10. Lee, *History of Hamilton County*, 1:133–34.

Bibliography

Andreas, A. T. *Illustrated Historical Atlas of the State of Iowa.* Chicago: Andreas Atlas Co., 1875.

Atherton, Lewis E. *The Pioneer Merchant in Mid-America.* Columbia: University of Missouri Press, 1939.

Bogue, Allan G. *From Prairie to Corn Belt: Farming on the Illinois and Iowa Prairies in the Nineteenth Century.* Chicago: University of Chicago Press, 1963.

———. "Pioneer Farmers and Innovation." *Iowa Journal of History* 56 (January 1958): 1–36.

The census returns of the different counties of the state of Iowa in 1856, showing in detail, the population, place of nativity, agricultural statistics, domestic and general manufactures. Iowa City, Ia.: Crum & Boyce, 1857.

Crisis: A New Church Weekly and Family Periodical (LaPorte, Ind.), 1860.

Ekstrom, Doris Williams. Duncombe, Iowa. Interviews and correspondence with editor. February 1983 through October 1985.

Folmar, John Kent, ed. *From That Terrible Field: Civil War Letters of James M. Williams, Twenty-first Alabama Infantry Volunteers.* Tuscaloosa: University of Alabama Press, 1981.

———. "Pre–Civil War Sentiment from Belmont County: Correspondence of Hugh Anderson." *Ohio History* 78 (Summer 1969): 202–10, 229–30.

Ft. Dodge (Iowa) *Messenger*, November 1983.

Ft. Dodge (Iowa) *Messenger and Chronicle*, August 1935.

Ft. Dodge (Iowa) *Sentinel*, January 1859.

Gara, Larry. *The Liberty Line: The Legend of the Underground Railroad.* Lexington: University of Kentucky Press, 1961.

General Meeting of Receivers of the Heavenly Doctrines of the New Jerusalem, Held at Urbana, Ohio, Jan. 4–6, 1856. Boston: Otis Clapp, 1855.

Hafen, LeRoy R. *Colorado: The Story of a Western Commonwealth.* 1933. Reprint. New York: AMS, 1970.

"Homer, the First County Seat." Ft. Dodge *Messenger and Chronicle.*

Iowa. Department of Health, Vital Records Section. Certification of Death No. 10-80-78: John H. Williams. Des Moines, Iowa.

Iowa. Hamilton County. Deed Book 1. Recorders Office, Hamilton County Courthouse, Webster City, Iowa.

Iowa. Hamilton County. Deed Book of Plats 1. Recorders Office, Hamilton County Courthouse, Webster City, Iowa.

Iowa. Hamilton County. Town Lot Deed Book 1, Recorders Office, Hamilton County Courthouse, Webster City, Iowa.

"John F. Duncombe's 1856 Journal," Ft. Dodge *Messenger*, November 23, 24, 1983.

"Journal of the Annual Meeting of the Illinois Association of the New Jerusalem, held in the Temple in Canton, on the 19th, 20th, and 21st days of October, 1866." *The New Jerusalem Magazine* 39 (1866−67): 1−22.

Journal of the Fourteenth Annual Meeting of the New Church Western Convention, Held in Cincinnati, May 21, 1846. Boston: Otis Clapp, 1846.

Journal of the Fifteenth Annual Meeting of the New Church Western Convention, Held in Cincinnati, May 20, 1847. Boston: Otis Clapp, 1847.

Journal of the Sixteenth Annual Meeting of the New Church Western Convention, Held in Cincinnati, May 17, 1848. Boston: Otis Clapp, 1848.

Journal of the Proceedings of the New Church Held in Cincinnati, From Friday the 18th to Sunday the 20th of May, 1849. Boston: Otis Clapp, 1849.

Journal of Proceedings of the Ohio Association, August 29, 1856: Second Annual New Church Meeting of Ohio. Boston: Otis Clapp, 1856.

Journal of the Proceedings of the Thirty-fourth General Convention of the New Church in the United States. Boston: Otis Clapp, 1852.

Journal of the Second Annual Meeting of the Ohio Association, Held in Cincinnati, May 17, 1850. Boston: Otis Clapp, 1850.

"Journal of the Twenty-Fifth Annual Meeting of the Illinois Association of the New Jerusalem, held at the Temple in Peoria, on the 7th, 8th, and 9th days of October, 1864." *The New Jerusalem Magazine* 37 (1864−65): 1−21.

"Journal of the Twenty-Sixth Annual Meeting of the Illinois Association of the New Jerusalem, held in the Temple in Chicago, on the 6th, 7th, and 8th days of October, 1865." *The New Jerusalem Magazine* 38 (1865–66): 1–28.

Lee, J. W. *History of Hamilton County*, Iowa. 2 vols. Chicago: S. J. Clarke Co., 1912.

Lyon, Bessie L. *Early Days In Hamilton County.* Webster City, Ia.: Freeman-Journal Publishing Co., 1946.

———. "The Passing of Homer." *The Palimpsest* 3 (December 1922): 381–89.

Marold, Irene Williams. Saguache, Colorado. Interview with editor. February 9, 1983.

Minutes of the First Meeting of the Ohio Conference of the New Church, Held in Cincinnati, Ohio, on Saturday and Sunday, May 22 and 23, 1852. Boston: Otis Clapp, 1852.

Mobile (Ala.) *Daily Register,* 1903.

National Archives. Pension Records. Pension Application File 482846 [Joseph Parker Williams].

New Jerusalem Messenger 29 (November 1880).

Noble, Rev. Samuel. *An Appeal in Behalf of the Views of the Eternal World and State and the Doctrines of Faith and Life Held by the body of Christians who believe that a New Church is signified in the Revelation, . . . by the New Jerusalem. . . .* London: J. S. Hodson, 1826.

Ohio. Belmont County. Deed Book 39. Belmont County Courthouse, St. Clairsville, Ohio.

Parker, Nathan Howe. *Iowa As It Is in 1855: A Gazetteer for Citizens and a Handbook for Immigrants. . . .* Chicago: Keen and Lee, 1855.

Progressive Men of Western Colorado. Chicago: A. W. Bowen & Co., 1905.

Randall, James G., and David Donald. *The Civil War and Reconstruction.* Lexington, Mass.: D. C. Heath and Co., 1969.

Rieger, Paul E. Sylvania, Ohio. Letter to editor, November 19, 1969.

Ruggles, W. Oakley. "Early Recollections of Fort Dodge." *Iowa Journal of History* 49 (April 1951): 168–84.

Sage, Leland L. *A History of Iowa.* Ames: Iowa State University Press, 1974.

St. Clairsville (Ohio) *Gazette.* 1838–52, 1866, 1903.

Smith, Ophia D. "The New Jerusalem Church in Ohio from 1848 to 1870," *Ohio State Archaeological and Historical Journal* 62 (January 1953): 25–54.

Sutton, Eric A. *The Living Thoughts of Swedenborg.* London: Cassell and Company, 1947.

Swisher, Jacob A. "The Location of County Seats in Iowa." *Iowa Journal of History and Politics* 22 (April, July, 1924): 217–94, 323–62.

U.S. Bureau of the Census. Manuscript Census of Population, Hamilton and Webster Counties, Iowa. 1860–80, 1900, 1910.

Warner, Ezra J. *Generals in Blue: Lives of Union Commanders.* Baton Rouge: Louisiana State University Press, 1964.

Watts, Peter. *Dictionary of the Old West.* New York: Alfred A. Knopf, 1977.

Webster City (Iowa) *Daily Freeman-Journal*, July 1933.

Webster City (Iowa) *Hamilton Freeman,* 1857–61, 1880.

Williams, James Madison, Papers. In the possession of Mrs. Louise Chamberlin, Mobile, Alabama.

Zornow, William Frank. *Kansas: A History of the Jayhawk State.* Norman: University of Oklahoma Press, 1957.

Index

Blair, E. H., 13, 42, 55, 76, 85, 106
Brown, George, 16, 20, 63–64, 71, 73, 81, 88, 89, 92

Chancy, Hiram, 3, 106
Church, Jane, 8
Church, William L., 3, 6, 8, 48, 57, 79
Corbin, Dr. Hampson, 56, 74, 79
Cowan, D. D. T., 23, 45, 46, 47, 51, 54, 71

Dally, Henry, 45
Dally, John, 3
Daniels, Oscar J., 22
Daniels, William B., 25, 34, 63, 71, 81
Daniels, William R., 6, 79
DeWitt, Barnabas, 74, 79
DeWitt, George, 83
DeWitt, Jeptha, 74
DeWitt, Rachel, 83

Economic conditions (money, farming, cattle), 10–11, 15, 16–17, 24, 30, 44–45, 47, 51–52, 53–55, 60, 65–66, 73, 80–81, 86–87, 92–93, 98–99

Fisher, Richard, 5, 67
Ft. Pickens, 124

Gregory, George, 18, 74

Hall, James, 79

Hartman, James, 6, 8, 12, 13, 25, 42, 61, 79, 119
Hartman, Mary, 6, 8, 11, 31, 85, 118
Homer: conditions in, 3, 6, 7–8, 41, 74, 82; education, 37, 39, 42, 46–47, 59, 62, 74

Jackson, Rachel, 76, 103

McPheeters, Benjamin, 3, 13, 38
Maxwell, Judge John D., 72
Messemore, A., 18, 74
Miller, Gabriel, 106
Miller, J. J., 55, 62

Pemberton, Columbus, 7, 11, 31, 38, 67, 71, 76
Pemberton, Emily, 119
Pemberton, Emma, 21
Pemberton, H. C., 3, 62, 67, 79, 85, 103
Pemberton, J. W., 23
"Pikes Peakism," 24–25, 34–36, 37, 42, 61, 66, 67, 74, 94
Porterfield, Caroline, 5, 106
Porterfield, James, 68, 79

Shannon, Gov. Wilson, 25
Sibert, William, 79
Skinner, Jacob, 146
Smith, Electa, 8, 87, 106, 116
Smith, Elizabeth B., 125
Smith, J. S., 82, 90
Stephens, Alexander H., 113
Swanger, Drisilla, 6

Tucker, Sereptha, 7, 13

Williams, J. H.: politics, 111–114,
  127; Swedenborgian theology
  and advice to James, 7, 11–12,
  16, 32–33, 37–38, 40, 69–70,
  126–127
Wolsey, William F., 74

BUR OAK BOOKS

A Cook's Tour of Iowa
By Susan Puckett

Fragile Giants: A Natural History of the Loess Hills
By Cornelia F. Mutel

An Iowa Album: A Photographic History, 1860–1920
By Mary Bennett

Landforms of Iowa
By Jean C. Prior

More han Ola og han Per
By Peter J. Rosendahl

Neighboring on the Air: Cooking with the KMA Radio Homemakers
By Evelyn Birkby

Nineteenth-Century Home Architecture of Iowa City: A Silver Edition
By Margaret N. Keyes

Nothing to Do but Stay: My Pioneer Mother
By Carrie Young

Old Capitol: Portrait of an Iowa Landmark
By Margaret N. Keyes

Parsnips in the Snow: Talks with Midwestern Gardeners
By Jane Anne Staw and Mary Swander

A Place of Sense: Essays in Search of the Midwest
Edited by Michael Martone

A Ruth Suckow Omnibus
By Ruth Suckow

"A Secret to Be Burried": The Diary and Life of Emily Hawley Gillespie, 1858–1888
By Judy Nolte Lensink

Tales of an Old Horsetrader: The First Hundred Years
By Leroy Judson Daniels

The Tattooed Countess
By Carl Van Vechten

"This State of Wonders": The Letters of an Iowa Frontier Family, 1858–1861
Edited by John Kent Folmar

Vandemark's Folly
By Herbert Quick